Improve Quality & Productivity With Simulation

Improvements in quality and productivity require discovery and implementation of new ideas, methods, processes and actions. This demands that the performance of numerous alternatives be accurately predicted in terms of their ability to improve the efficiency, economy, and effectiveness of work. Simulation is a tool which can help make these predictions.

Improve Quality & Productivity With Simulation

Second Edition

Authors: Thomas J. Gogg and Jack R. A. Mott

Manufactured in the United States of America

10   9   8   7   6   5   4   3   2   1

Library of Congress Catalog Card Number: 92-85591

ISBN 1-882229-03-7

About The Authors.....

Thomas J. Gogg is Director of Engineering at JMI Consulting Group in Palos Verdes, California. His background includes eleven years of experience in Technical Staff positions in the manufacturing operations at Xerox Corporation and Hughes Aircraft Company. His past nine years have focused on the application of simulation in manufacturing and industry. He has given lectures at several simulation seminars, and has co-authored other books and articles on simulation including publication in the *Industrial Engineering* magazine and proceedings of the *Winter and Summer Simulation Conferences*. Tom is a corporate trainer and lecturer for the *American Management Association*. Tom is also the co-developer and co-author of the Simulation Scholar©, the Simulation Benefits Analyzer© and the Simulation Output Analyzer©. Tom received a B.S. degree in Industrial Engineering from Iowa State University.

Jack R. A. Mott M.B.A., C.P.A. is President of JMI Consulting Group in Palos Verdes, California. Prior to forming JMI in 1988, he had thirteen years of experience at Arthur Andersen & Co., Levi Strauss, Inc., and Xerox Corporation. He has held management positions in Manufacturing, Finance, and Marketing and Sales. Jack holds a B.S. in Accounting/Economics from Loyola University and an M.B.A. degree from Loyola Marymount University. He is also a licensed Certified Public Accountant. He has given lectures at several simulation seminars, and has co-authored other books and articles on simulation including publication in the *Industrial Engineering* magazine and proceedings of the *Winter and Summer Simulation Conferences*. Jack is a corporate trainer and lecturer for the *American Management Association*. Jack is also the co-developer and co-author of the Simulation Scholar©, the Simulation Benefits Analyzer© and the Simulation Output Analyzer©. He is fluent in the Spanish language and has conducted business in Japan, Europe, South America and Mexico.

Acknowledgments...

JMI Consulting Group would like to thank the following people who have contributed their time, and expertise. Your contributions were greatly appreciated.

H. Wayne Andrews	Bob Hoyt
Jim Archer	Kathi Hunt
Brad Armstrong	Cliff King
Roger Beadle	Patrick Maroney
Willi Bernhard	Deborah Mott
Roger Biggeln	Maureen McQuaid
Dan Brown	Scott Nalick
Daniel T. Brunner	Brian O'Neill
Jodi Claassen	David Profozich
Kevin Cotner	Charles D. Sands
Alice Cox	Dave Sly
Dave Crahl	Karen Stanley
Katherine Drury	Roger Swanson
Robert Edsall	Scott Swegles
Susan Emens	Kerim (Ken) Tumay
Joesph R. Flemming	Marc Ulbrich
Earl J. Gantz	Larry Violante
Mary Gogg	Jim Vaughn
Winston Hait	Caroline Zenkevich

Preface

Improve Quality and Productivity! This is the "battle cry" of the nineties. Those that achieve this goal will become leaders. Those who do not will become casualties of an increasingly competitive market.

Strategies for radical, fundamental, or continuous improvements are being implemented across all industries. Business Process Reengineering, Total Quality Management, Continuous Measurable Improvement, and Statistical Process Control are just a few of the many techniques being applied. They all have as an essential element the need to evaluate ideas for improvement. In other words, one must be able to predict the performance of alternatives in order to make wise decisions. Simulation is one of the best instruments for predicting outcomes for possible alternative courses of action. It is a dynamic decision-making tool which can help expedite the transformation to continual improvement. ***Simulation is the bridge between ideas and implementation.***

Many businesses are uncertain about what simulation is, why it is needed, how it works, and how it can save them money. Many are failing to grasp the multitude of benefits it can provide. Potential dollar savings are not being realized. ***Simulation education is the first step towards solving this problem.***

The purpose of this book is to give the reader a quick overview of fundamental principles, methodology, procedures, software, mathematics, and benefits associated with simulation modeling. It is particularly useful as a presentation tool for simulation users and non-simulation users who are trying to 1) introduce simulation to an organization or 2) educate personnel involved with a simulation project. It can also be used as a textbook for educators who teach simulation as part of another course in engineering, management and business programs.

Building credibility into models is a primary objective of simulation users. This is accomplished by ensuring that all people contributing to a study and all who will be affected by the results (managers, engineers, financial and operational personnel) have a basic understanding of what simulation is, why it is being used, and how it works. Part of this book is devoted to assessing the savings from a simulation investment. It provides detailed cost, benefit and payback information for supporting an investment in simulation.

Elementary training for people directly or indirectly involved with simulation is a vital and critical step in any simulation project. Unfortunately, it is usually by-passed. A brief, informative training session at the onset of a project can be the difference between success and failure. This book is designed in an instructional format conducive to this type of training. Educational tools including the ***Simulation Scholar©***, a Windows based interactive tutorial and reference, and presentation kits including visual transparencies of all tables, charts and graphs, plus trainer tools are available through JMI Consulting Group, 2516 Via Tejon Suite 310, Palos Verdes Estates, CA 90274, Tel: (310) 373-6540 Fax: (310) 373-0772.

Simulation Of A Blank Page

TABLE OF CONTENTS

TABLE OF CONTENTS

TABLE OF CONTENTS

TABLE OF CONTENTS

TABLE OF CONTENTS

Chapter 1

WHAT IS SIMULATION?

What Is Simulation?

- Simulation Is Experimenting With A Model

- Simulation Is A Problem-Solving Tool

- Simulation Modeling In The Past

- Simulation Modeling Today And Tomorrow

Simulation Is Experimenting With A Model

Ask people to define simulation and you will probably discover that the majority can not. Simulation has been successfully utilized for many years, yet few people have a thorough understanding of what it is or how it works. It is not as complicated as many believe it to be. *"Simulation is the use of a model (not necessarily a computer model) to conduct experiments which, by inference, convey an understanding of the behavior of the system modeled. Computer modeling is the programming of a computer to produce a system surrogate having variables whose values over time are determined by the same laws of dynamics as the variables of a real-world or hypothesized system"* [McLeod (1988)]. A shorter definition is, **"Simulation is the art and science of creating a representation of a process or system for the purpose of experimentation and evaluation."**

The purpose of experimenting is to discover something unknown or to test a hypothesis. It can yield a greater understanding of the potential consequences associated with different courses of action. Understanding these consequences can help ensure wise decisions. It is essential that right decisions be made the first time in today's economic climate. Proceeding with questionable designs and uncertain solutions is very risky. Testing alternatives through experimentation is a logical approach for reducing the uncertainty associated with a candidate solution. The experience gained from experimentation can help avoid unnecessary and costly ventures.

Simulation Is A Problem-Solving Tool

Simulation is a tool which can help solve problems. A problem arises from any question or matter involving doubt, uncertainty or difficulty. For many problems there can be an infinite number of possible solutions. Finding potential solutions first requires a thorough understanding of what constitutes the problem. This is achieved by collecting and analyzing data pertaining to it. Candidate solutions are based on results obtained from these actions. **Simulation is a tool which helps analyze the facts and conditions associated with a problem**.

One of the final steps in any problem-solving process is to make a decision as to which candidate solution is optimal with respect to a desired outcome. The decision-making phase of the problem-solving process requires the following three steps: (1) criteria must be selected and their relative weights determined; (2) performance of candidate solutions must be predicted with respect to the criteria; and (3) the candidates must be compared on the basis of these predicted performances [Krick (1976)]. **Simulation helps find candidate solutions and provides a means for evaluating them**.

Wisdom needs to be applied whenever decisions are made. In terms of problem-solving, wisdom means selecting a course of action which will have the highest probability of achieving a desired result. Good decision-making is based on the precept of prediction. **Simulation is one of the best instruments for predicting performances. It turns data into knowledge, and knowledge into experience**.

WHAT IS SIMULATION?

Simulation Modeling In The Past

Computer simulation modeling came to age in the late 1950's. It typically fell under the domain of operations research and management sciences. In the past, it was only used as a last resort when a complex system could not be studied in any other manner. The simulation process was usually very time-consuming and required high budgets for lengthy computer processing times. Output reports were often difficult to interpret and communicate.

Simulation users required a strong computer programming background. Approximately forty percent or more of the simulation effort was consumed by programming related tasks. **Model verification** (Is the model operating in the manner intended?) and **model validation** (Is the model accurately reflecting the system under study?) typically demanded exhausting hours interpreting endless pages of computer coding and output. The time spent experimenting with a model was normally limited due to the costs associated with making changes (See Charts C1A and C1B).

TASK TIME ALLOCATIONS
Expressed As A Percentage Of Total Time Spent
Collecting Data, Building A Model, And Experimenting With It

Chart C1A   Simulation In The **Past**

Collecting Data (40%)
Building Model (50%)
Experimenting With Model (10%)

Chart C1B   Simulation **Today**

Collecting Data (40%)
Building Model (20%)
Experimenting With Model (40%)

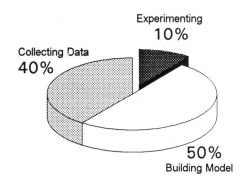

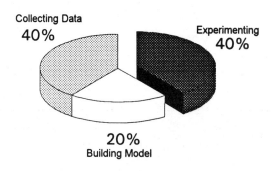

Simulation Modeling Today And Tomorrow

Today's simulation products have significantly reduced the programming effort in the model building process. Computer programming skills, although beneficial, are no longer mandatory. PC-based simulation products eliminate the runtime costs incurred with mainframe computers. Graphical animation features make model verification much simpler. Communicating system flows and conveying results are significantly embellished.

Menu-driven input screens are common with many packages. They reduce the time required to build models. Some possess quick model interaction capabilities. Changes can be readily incorporated into active simulations and their resulting impacts can be immediately observed. More time can be allocated to experimenting with "what-if" scenarios.

The increased role of simulation in problem-solving is inevitable. Application areas continue to expand. Business process reengineering, manufacturing, chemical and food processing, distribution systems, transportation, service industries, military, communicaton systems and computer systems are all viable candidates for simulation analyses. **Unfortunately, simulation technology has advanced further and more quickly than the communication of its prowess as a problem-solving tool. Realization of its benefits will largely depend upon eliminating the fears and unfamiliarities often associated with it**.

Simulation Of A Blank Page

Chapter 2

WHY SIMULATE?

IMPROVE QUALITY & PRODUCTIVITY WITH SIMULATION

Why Simulate?

- Simulation Can Predict Outcomes For Possible Courses of Action

- Simulation Can Account For The Effects Of Variances Occurring In A Process Or System

- Simulation Promotes Total Solutions

- Simulation Brings Expertise Knowledge And Information Together

- Simulation Can Be Cost Effective In Terms Of Time

- Simulation Can Foster Creative Attitudes And A Zeal For Trying New Ideas

Simulation Can Predict Outcomes For Possible Courses Of Action

"Management of a system is action based on prediction. Rational prediction requires systematic learning and comparisons of predictions of short-term and long-term results of possible alternative courses of action" [Deming (1989)]. Simulation educates people on how a system operates. It is an excellent tool for forecasting outcomes. Alternative courses of action can be readily tested to determine their effects on system performances.

Testing is a natural prerequisite to implementation. It helps guarantee success. Experimenting with the "real thing" is the ultimate means of testing. Unfortunately, this is rarely feasible. **As the cost of a proposed solution increases, so does the cost of physically experimenting with it**.

Suppose a new, large scale conveyor system is being considered as an alternative for improving productivity. It would not be cost effective to install this system and then determine whether or not it is a good solution. Experimenting with a representation (model) of the system is a better way to find out.

Most of today's systems are dynamic and stochastic in nature. A dynamic system implies action. Factors that influence a system can change as time progresses (a manufacturing system is subjected to part scheduling changes, equipment breakdowns, part defects, etc.). Stochastic suggests that these changes can vary indiscriminately. Some examples of stochastic factors are displayed in Table T2A on page 2-4.

Three types of models are often employed when evaluating potential improvements proposed for dynamic/stochastic systems. They are 1) opinion models, 2) static mathematical models, and 3) simulation models.

<u>Opinion models</u> are composed primarily of assumptions. They tend to test egos rather than solutions feasibility. The beliefs and ideas of an individual or group of individuals serve as a representation of a system. Little or no quantifiable data is used to evaluate alternatives.

<u>Static mathematical models</u> delineate a system mathematically. The operational characteristics of a system are described in terms of numerical equations. The potential effects of an alternative are derived from a single computation of the equations. The variable values used in the computation are constants based on averages. System behavior and performance are determined by summing individual effects. Spreadsheet analyses are an example of static mathematical models.

<u>Simulation models</u> are also mathematical in nature and employ the use of numerical equations to describe a system's operational characteristics. **Simulation models differ from static models because they are event driven** (An event is something that happens. A part arriving at a machine can be thought of as an event). The occurrence of an event can change the values of the variables used in a computation. System behavior and performance are derived by averaging the responses observed over the occurrences of a large quantity of events.

Table T2A Examples Of Random Occurring Events

- Schedule Changes
- Equipment Failures
- Customer Arrivals Into A System
- Defect/Scrap Rates
- Absenteeism
- Wait Time Between Operations

- Engineering Changes
- Test Times
- New Product Development Times
- Operation Cycle Times
- Material Shortages
- Repair Times

Problems which surface in dynamic/stochastic systems typically become more difficult to analyze as the number of stochastic variables and interdependencies/interrelationships multiply. Graph C2A depicts this correlation. Abstracting the essence of a problem and its underlying structure grows more difficult with each additional variable. Gaining insight to cause-and-effect relationships and their magnitudes can be a formidable task. Simulation is a tool that is well-suited for addressing the synergetic response of multiple variables within a system. The insights that can be obtained from using it normally increase as the number of system variables and interdependencies escalate.

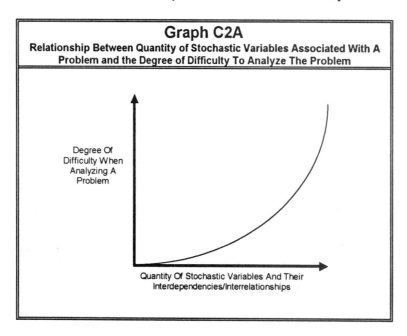

Graph C2A
Relationship Between Quantity of Stochastic Variables Associated With A Problem and the Degree of Difficulty To Analyze The Problem

Degree Of Difficulty When Analyzing A Problem

Quantity Of Stochastic Variables And Their Interdependencies/Interrelationships

Table T2B on page 2-5 illustrates the relationship between model types (opinion, static mathematical and simulation) and their ability to analyze dynamic/stochastic systems. The benefits gained are directly related to a model's capacity to produce responses that are reflective of the actual responses produced or expected by the system being studied. Simulation models are generally superior imitators of dynamic/stochastic systems when compared to static mathematical models or opinion models.

Table T2B	
Model Type	**Ability To Analyze Stochastic/Dynamic Systems**
Opinion Models	**LOW**
Static Mathematical Models	**MEDIUM**
Simulation Models	**HIGH**

Simulation Can Account For The Effects Of Variances Occurring In A Process Or System

Simulation can account for the effects of variances occurring within a system (a variance implies that something changes from one incident to another). Conventional analytical methods, such as static mathematical models, do not effectively address this issue. Performance calculations derived from them are generally based on constant values, and the constant values are based on averages. An average production rate of four hundred parts per month, an average time between failures of 60 hours, and an average assembly cycle time of two hours are typical examples. Performance computations based solely on mean values neglect the effect of variances. Disregarding this factor can lead to erroneous conclusions.

Static mathematical models downplay the impact of stochastic processes even though they exist in almost all systems. They overlook the role of *time* when analyzing a problem. What is the impact when something occurs in relation to other incidents? What if a machine malfunctions at a time when no labor is available to repair it? The fact that a machine is non-producing an average of ten percent of its total operating time does not account for the repercussions that might occur based on **when** it is non-producing. The consequences of breaking down are greater during peak production demands than during low production demands.

A common performance index used in many manufacturing systems is centered around a ratio of actual hours spent, to standard hours earned. In a utopian system, the ratio should always be equal to one. However, this rarely occurs. Performance fluctuates with time. It rises and falls continuously. When it falls below a specified limit, analyses are quickly initiated to discover the cause for the decrease. The problems revealed are usually associated with the occurrences of random events.

WIP (Work-In-Process) levels are a classical example of a performance criterion that can be heavily influenced by variances. Fluctuations in operation cycle times between consecutive operations can increase WIP levels and prolong wait time in queues (non-value-added time).

Simulation can be very effective for deriving solutions that will minimize the impact of variances, or eliminate them entirely. It assesses the ramifications of random changes occurring in a system relative to some objective. **The interrelational characteristics and interdependencies of people, equipment, methods and material are examined as they evolve through time. The behavior of a system is described in terms of discrete, and/or continuous events occurring within it**. Table T2C displays some elementary questions which help define the interrrelational characteristics and interdependencies in a process or system.

Table T2C
Questions For Defining Interrelationships And Interdependencies Of Elements In A System
• What type of labor, equipment, or material is needed to perform the operations and processes that compose a system?
• When are the equipment, labor, and material required to perform the operations and processes that exist in a system needed?
• Where does the material, labor, and equipment that support the operations and processes within a system come from?
• What rules govern the movement of equipment, labor and material throughout a process or system?
• What conditions can influence the performance of labor, equipment, or any other element within a process or system?

Problem-solvers cannot control the occurrences of random events. However, they can predict the consequences of these events and their likelihood of occurrence. With this information, efforts can be focused on maximizing a system's efficiency by 1) reducing the likelihood of random events, and/or 2) minimizing the impact from random events. Simulation gives a problem-solver a tool for measuring the effectiveness of solutions created by these efforts.

Simulation Promotes Total Solutions

A total solution is a complete solution. A problem is eliminated rather than passed along. For example, WIP problems in one area of a manufacturing process are often solved by passing the problem to the next operation in the process. A total solution benefits an entire system, not just a portion of a system.

Simulation is an excellent tool for analyzing entire problems and finding total solutions. It is based on the principle of synergism. **Synergism** is defined as the simultaneous actions of separate elements within a system which together have greater total effect on system performance than the sum of their individual effects.

Many problem-solving approaches try to analyze problems by dissecting them into sub-problems. The sub-problems are frequently categorized according to departments affiliated with the issues. Quality problems, process problems, engineering problems, and test problems are a few examples. Each department tries to solve its portion of a problem independently. This practice often yields fragmented solutions rather than an overall complete solution. **Total solutions are more likely to be found when a total problem is analyzed as a whole. Simulation promotes this type of analysis.**

Simulation Brings Expertise, Knowledge And Information Together

Improvements in quality and productivity are usually pursued through a variety of strategies. JIT (Just In Time), TQM (Total Quality Management), SPC (Statistical Process Control), and BPR (Business Process Reengineering) strategists are all pursuing the goals of their respective disciplines. Sometimes, each faction strives to function independently of the others. This can lead to competitive, rather than cooperative actions between groups. **The simulation modeling building process can help unite the ideas and proficiencies of numerous people.**

When executed properly, the simulation process brings together a broad scope of knowledge, information and expertise from a variety of sources. The questions, problems and concerns from multiple viewpoints are unveiled. A better comprehension of a total system is gained because the interdependencies of all components are shared and understood by all parties contributing input to a model. People become a team working together towards a common goal.

The sharing of information across diversified groups is an important and necessary component in all world class management strategies. Good communication and cooperation between people are mandatory for making continual improvements in quality and productivity. There must be a united interest in a product, and a dedicated commitment to better the process that makes it. Simulation is a tool that can help inspire this interest and commitment.

Simulation Can Be Cost Effective In Terms Of Time

Simulation can produce savings in terms of time. PC-based simulation packages have eliminated high computer processing costs. The time required to build models has been considerably reduced. The data collection effort needed to create credible simulation models is the same as the effort needed with static mathematical models or other analytical approaches.

Organizations must be able to react quickly to changes. A validated simulation model is an excellent tool for rapidly analyzing future changes. It already contains the ground structure for processing information in terms of performance criteria. The time, effort, and costs associated with reestablishing that structure do not have to be reincurred when evaluating future alternatives.

Simulation has proven to be an excellent educational tool. It is a common communicator that creates experience. Experience produces knowledge, and knowledge is money. The operational characteristics of a system can be learned much faster with a simulation model as compared to a learn-as-you-go type philosophy. Less time is required for teaching people about the dynamics of a process or system. **The time required to communicate ideas is also significantly reduced.** The cliché, "A picture paints a thousand words," is a good way to describe the difference between the communication capabilities of static analyses and simulation. <u>**A spreadsheet full of numbers does not wield the communication power of visual animation.**</u>

The simulation benefits described to this point have not been quantified in terms of dollars. A simulation investment is usually contingent upon some type of financial justification. The monetary savings gained from an investment in simulation must be greater than the cost of obtaining them. Chapter 14, *"Assessing Savings From A Simulation Investment"* provides additional information for presenting the cost savings that can be achieved from an investment in simulation.

Simulation Can Foster Creative Attitudes And A Zeal For Trying New Ideas

Many companies have under-utilized resources, which if fully employed, can bring about dramatic improvements in quality and productivity. The knowledge, ideas, and creativity of employees are prime examples. Ideas that can produce considerable improvements are often never tried because of an employee's fear of failure -- an outlook of "I think this might work, but I am not going to try it because it might fail." Simulation can help change this sentiment. It encourages optimism and creative attitudes: "I think this might work, so let's test it and find out." <u>**A simulation model can be a thorough and economical way to express, experiment with, and evaluate ideas.**</u>

The next chapter, *"How Does Simulation Work,"* explains a mathematical exercise that illustrates **HOW** simulation computes the metrics (measurements of effectiveness) associated with a candidate solution. When reading this topic, keep in mind that the exercise is **NOT** intended as an example of the actions needed to build a simulation model. Its purpose is to demonstrate the mathematics involved with simulation.

Chapter 3

HOW DOES SIMULATION WORK?

How Does Simulation Work?

- Using Mathematical Variables To Describe The Metrics Of A System

- Using Mathematics To Simulate A Simple System

Using Mathematical Variables To Describe The Metrics Of A System

Metrics are a major component of most analytical studies. Metrics refer to the describing of a problem, process, or system in terms of measurements. Mathematical variables can be used to quantify the characteristics of a system. For example, elements within a system can often be described in terms of quantifiable variables. The cycle time for a part on a certain machine might be represented by a variable called **CTIME**. The variable **TPARTS** can represent the total parts produced in **2000** working hours. It can be mathematically expressed as **TPARTS=2000 ÷ CTIME**.

Variables can assume any given value or collection of values. Their values can change according to a set of rules or instructions. An instruction can be as simple as the following: If **TPARTS** is greater than **1000** then a variable called **EXCESS** is equal to **TPARTS** minus **1000**. In terms of a mathematical instruction it can be described as follows: **IF TPARTS > 1000** then **EXCESS=TPARTS - 1000**. Suppose **TPARTS=1500**. The value for **EXCESS** would then equal **500**. It would be calculated as **EXCESS=1500 - 1000**.

Discrete event simulation modeling is the processing of a repetitive set of instructions. The instructions define how the values for variables can change in relation to changing conditions. Conditions change because of the occurrences of events. A part arriving at a machine or part leaving a machine can be considered an event. A machine breakdown is another example of an event. As each event occurs, a set of actions (computations) is performed pertaining to it.

A dynamic (things change with respect to time) and discrete event (things occur at unique points in time) simulation model performs a repetitious sequence of instructions similar to the following: 1) Determine what event type will occur next, 2) Set a simulation clock variable equal to the time of the next event 3) Update any statistical variables where required, 4) Perform the actions (computations) associated with the most current event, and 5) Schedule a time for the next occurrence of that event type.

Using Mathematics To Simulate A Simple System

It is now possible to build models with little or no knowledge of the code-writing logistics, or the mathematics involved with simulation. However, it is still beneficial for simulation users, management, and project participants to have an elementary appreciation of the principles governing the reasoning and computations used with simulation. Results can be misinterpreted when their derivations are not understood.

Suppose an employee analyzes a problem and then gives his or her manager a piece of paper containing a recommended solution. The manager will probably be more willing to accept that solution if he or she has a basic understanding of how it was derived. The same principle applies to people who are involved with a simulation project, and to those who will be affected by its results.

A reason often heard for not giving elementary simulation education to operational personnel (and sometimes management) is, "It's too complicated. They will not understand it." The phrase "simulation modeling" still carries an unjust connotation of being complicated. In reality, it is fairly straightforward: **Define** the problem; **Collect** and **Analyze** data pertaining to the problem (build a mathematical representation of the problem); **Search** for solutions; **Evaluate** and **Select** a solution; and **Implement** the solution. <u>**A simulation user's most formidable task is often associated with educating others about the methodologies and benefits of simulation.**</u>

Consider a simple system consisting of three entities: 1) parts, 2) a machine, and 3) a queueing buffer (A queue indicates a waiting line. A queueing buffer refers to a place where parts can accumulate prior to being processed at the machine). There are two event types: 1) a part arrives at the queueing buffer and 2) a part leaves the machine. The time between part arrivals in the queueing buffer changes randomly. It is either **1**, **2**, **3**, **4**, **5**, or **6** minutes. The probability of occurrence is the same for all six values. Each part is processed individually at the machine. The machine cycle time per part is also random. Its possible values are again **1**, **2**, **3**, **4**, **5**, or **6** minutes, each with an equal probability of occurrence. Suppose we need to <u>estimate the average number of parts that can be expected in the queueing buffer during a given time interval</u>. How would you solve this problem?

One approach might be to physically recreate the scenario and manually record the average time each part spends in the queue. Another approach is to recreate the sequence of events experienced in the system by means of mathematics. The latter method would probably be less costly than the first.

The following exercise (Exercise 3A) demonstrates a mathematical representation of the previously described queueing system. Stepping through the exercise will illustrate the type of reasoning and logic involved with discrete event simulation modeling. Table 3A (page 3-6) contains a list of mathematical variables that have been created for describing the various entities and characteristics of the system. Pages 3-9 through 3-14 contain six sets of instructions. They are:

1) **Initializing System Variables**   4) **Creating A Variable Status Report**
2) **Determining Next Event Types**   5) **Processing A Part Arrival Event**
3) **Updating Statistical Variables**   6) **Processing A Part Departure Event**

A series of actions are described in each instruction set. These actions primarily involve 1) performing simple mathematical computations using different variable values in Table 3A (page 3-6), and 2) recording the results in either of two tables (Table 3A, page 3-6 and Table 3B, page 3-12).

The flow chart on page 3-5 illustrates the sequence in which the instruction sets are performed. During the exercise, variables in Table 3A will change values as the various instruction sets are concluded. For example, the exercise begins by performing the actions described in the instructions for "**Initializing System Variables**" (page 3-9). The chart titled, "**Step 1-Initializing System Variables**," on page 3-7 depicts the status of Table 3A before and after the actions of this instruction set are performed.

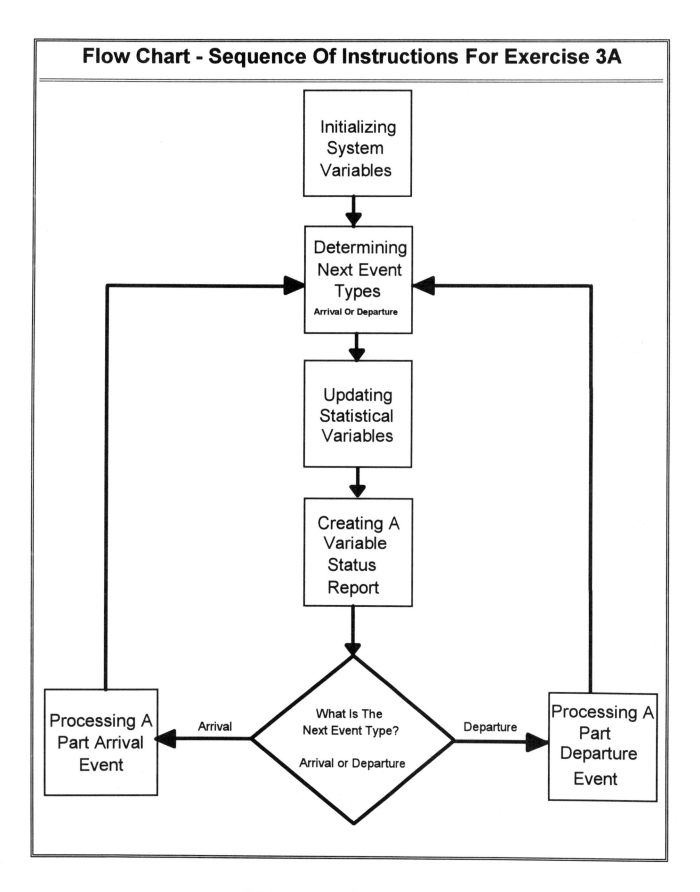

Flow Chart - Sequence Of Instructions For Exercise 3A

Initializing System Variables

Determining Next Event Types
Arrival Or Departure

Updating Statistical Variables

Creating A Variable Status Report

What Is The Next Event Type?
Arrival or Departure

Arrival

Departure

Processing A Part Arrival Event

Processing A Part Departure Event

Variable Status Table 3A

Simulation Clock Variable
CLOCK is a variable which represents simulated time in the exercise. It can be thought of as a mathematical clock which is updated each time an event occurs. An event in this exercise is the arrival of a part into the queueing buffer, or a departure of a part from the machine.

CLOCK= _____

Machine State Variable
MACHST is a variable which tells us the current state of the machine at any point in the exercise. If the machine is processing a part, then its state is BUSY. If it is not processing a part, then its state is IDLE.

MACHST= _____

Number Of Parts In Queue
NPIQ is a variable which represents the current number of parts which are waiting in the queue. If a part arrives and MACHST=BUSY, then NPIQ is incremented by 1. When a part departure event occurs, NPIQ is decreased by 1 if the value of NPIQ is greater than 0.

NPIQ= _____

Next Part Arrival Time
NPAT is a variable which tells us the future time of the next part arrival into the queueing buffer. It is calculated by adding the result of a die roll to the current value of the clock variable.

NPAT= _____

Next Part Departure Time
NPDT is a variable which tells us the point in future time that a part will depart the machine. It is calculated by adding a machine cycle (derived by rolling a die) to the current value of the clock variable.

NPDT _____

Total Parts Machined
TPM is a variable which records the total number of parts which have been machined. Each time a part departure event occurs, the TPM variable is incremented by 1.

TPM= _____

Total Parts Arrived
TPA is a variable which counts the total parts that have entered the queueing buffer. Each time a part arrival event occurs, the TPA variable is incremented by 1.

TPA= _____

Maximum Parts In Queue
MPIQ is a variable which carries the value for the maximum number of parts which exist in the queuing buffer during the exercise. The value for MPIQ is checked during each part arrival event. If MPIQ is less than NPIQ, then MPIQ is given the value of NPIQ.

MPIQ= _____

Time Of Last Event
TOLE is a variable which records the simulated clock time when the last event occurred (part arrival or part departure)

TOLE= _____

Time Since Last Event
TSLE is a variable which tells us how much simulated time has expired since the last part arrival or departure.

TSLE= _____

Cumulative Part-Minutes In Queue
CPMIQ is a variable which cumulates the total time spent by parts in the queueing buffer. The value for NPIQ multiplied by the value of TSLE tells us the total part minutes spent in the queueing buffer. It is calculated after each part arrival or departure. The result is added to the current value of CMPIQ.

CPMIQ _____

Average Queue Length
AVGQL is a variable which tells us the average part queue length in the queueing buffer. It is calculated by dividing CMPIQ by the current value for CLOCK.

AVGQL= _____

Event Type (Arrival or Departure)
ETYPE is a variable whose value determines whether a part arrival event is going to occur, or a part departure event is going to occur. It is dependent upon the value of NPAT and NPDT. If the value for NPAT is less than the value for NPDT, then ETYPE is equal to ARV.

ETYPE= _____

Step 1: Initializing System Variables

Initialize the values of the variables in Table 3A: CLOCK=0; MACHST=IDLE; NPIQ=0; NPAT=0; NPDT=NS; TPM=0; TPA=0; MPIQ=0; TOLE=0; TSLE=0; CPMIQ=0; AVGQL=0; ETYPE=NONE

(Before the instructions are performed)

Variable Status Table 3A

Simulation Clock Variable	CLOCK=
Machine State Variable	MACHST=
Number of Parts In Queue	NPIQ=
Next Part Arrival Time	NPAT=
Next Part Departure Time	NPDT=
Total Parts Machined	TPM=
Total Parts Arrived	TPA=
Maximum Parts In Queue	MPIQ=
Time of Last Event	TOLE=
Time Since Last Event	TSLE=
Cumulative Part-Minutes In Queue	CPMIQ=
Average Queue Length	AVGQL=
Event Type (Arrival or Departure)	ETYPE=

(After the instructions are performed)

Variable Status Table 3A

Simulation Clock Variable	CLOCK=	0
Machine State Variable	MACHST=	IDLE
Number of Parts In Queue	NPIQ=	0
Next Part Arrival Time	NPAT=	0
Next Part Departure Time	NPDT=	NS
Total Parts Machined	TPM=	0
Total Parts Arrived	TPA=	0
Maximum Parts In Queue	MPIQ=	0
Time of Last Event	TOLE=	0
Time Since Last Event	TSLE=	0
Cumulative Part-Minutes In Queue	CPMIQ=	0
Average Queue Length	AVGQL=	0
Event Type (Arrival or Departure)	ETYPE=	NONE

The final instruction in each instruction set directs the user to the next set of instructions to be performed. In this case, the user would go to the instructions for "**Determining Next Event Types**" (page 3-10).

As the exercise progresses, selected variable values from Table 3A are recorded in Table 3B (page 3-12) each time the actions for "**Creating A Variable Status Report**" are completed. **The contents of Table 3B are representative of output data produced by simulation. Average queue lengths and other system statistics (Total Parts Arrived, Total Parts Machined, Computer Clock Time, etc.) are displayed as a result of each part arrival or departure.** Data is currently exhibited in the first five rows. It is the result of performing the first twenty sets of instructions.

Many readers may not have the time to work through the instruction sets of Exercise 3A. Appendix A contains the calculations and ensuing results after performing each of the first twenty steps associated with this exercise. It is recommended that the reader review these results in order to gain a better understanding of the mathematics and logic involved with simulation modeling.

If desired, all or part of the remaining five rows in Table 3B can be completed by the reader. A roll of a die can be used to establish the respective random values associated with each part interarrival time and machine cycle duration. The results will be unique to the values obtained from the rolls of the die (Computer simulation utilizes probability distributions to imitate random behavior in a system. Chapters 6 through 8 provide more information on this subject).

The intent of Exercise 3A is to demonstrate basic procedures and computations used to mathematically simulate the aforementioned system. Determination of the long-term average queue length would require the reader to perform thousands of repetitive calculations. Appendix A, page A-13, contains a simple computer program for performing these tasks. Executing this program will step the user through the previously described instruction sets. It will also reveal that the average queue length will continue to increase as the simulation clock time progresses. (Analyses of queue lengths and wait times are further discussed in chapter 13 "*Where Can Simulation Be Used*?").

Manually performing repetitive actions involving numerous computations is not economical in terms of time or cost. Computers have eliminated this problem. Their drawback in the past was in the effort required to translate the actions (instructions) into a computer language. In the early days of simulation, this was usually a formidable task. Today this is not true. **The translation (code writing) process has been substantially simplified (in some cases almost eliminated) with most of today's simulation packages. This is why simulation is now a practical tool for problem-solving.**

Instructions For Initializing System Variables

1. Initialize the variables in Table 3A on page 3-6 with the following values:

- Set initial value for Simulation Clock variable to 0 — **CLOCK=0**

- Set initial value for Machine State variable to IDLE — **MACHST=IDLE**

- Set initial value for
  Number of Parts In Queueing Buffer to 0 — **NPIQ=0**

- Set value of Next Part Arrival Time variable equal to 0 — **NPAT=0**

- Set value of Next Part Departure Time variable
  equal to None Scheduled (NS) — **NPDT=NS**

- Set initial value for Total Parts Machined variable to 0 — **TPM=0**

- Set initial value for Total Parts Arrived variable to 0 — **TPA=0**

- Set initial value for Maximum Parts In Queue variable to 0 — **MPIQ=0**

- Set initial value for Time of Last Event variable to 0 — **TOLE=0**

- Set initial value for Time Since Last Event variable to 0 — **TSLE=0**

- Set initial value for Cumulative Part-Minutes
  In the Queueing Buffer variable to 0 — **CPMIQ=0**

- Set initial value for Average Number of Parts
  In the Queueing Buffer per variable to 0 — **AVGQL=0**

- Set initial value for the **Next Event Type**
  variable to NONE — **ETYPE=NONE**

2. Do the instructions for **Determining Next Event Types** on page 3-10

Instructions For Determining Next Event Types

Check Table 3A to determine the next event type (arrival or departure) that will occur. The decision is based on the values of Next Part Arrival Time (NPAT) and Next Part Departure Time (NPDT). An arrival event is selected if the value of NPAT is less than the value of NPDT or if there is no NPDT scheduled (NPDT=NS).

1.

IF

Next Part Arrival Time < Next Part Departure Time
NPAT < NPDT
or
Next Part Departure Time=None Scheduled
NPDT = NS

⇦⇦⇦NO⇦⇦⇦   ⇨⇨⇨YES⇨⇨⇨

NO	YES
2. Set the value of the simulation clock variable (CLOCK) in Table 3A equal to the current value of the Next Part Departure Time (NPDT). **CLOCK=NPDT**	**2.** Set the value of the simulation clock variable (CLOCK) in Table 3A equal to the current value of the Next Part Arrival Time (NPAT). **CLOCK=NPAT**
3. Set the value of variable ETYPE (Event Type) in Table 3A equal to DEP. **ETYPE=DEP**	**3.** Set the value of variable ETYPE (Event Type) in Table 3A equal to ARV. **ETYPE=ARV**
4. Go to the instructions for **Updating Statistical Variables** on page 3-11.	**4.** Go to the instructions for **Updating Statistical Variables** on page 3-11.

Instructions For Updating Statistical Variables

Update the following variables in Table 3A

1. Update the Time Since Last Event variable (TSLE). The time since the last event is equal to the current clock value (CLOCK) minus the time for the occurrence of the last event (TOLE)

$$TSLE=CLOCK-TOLE$$

2. Update the value for the Time Of The Last Event variable (TOLE). It is equal to the current value of the variable CLOCK.

$$TOLE=CLOCK$$

3. Cumulate the total number of part-minutes that have been experienced in the queueing buffer. The part-minutes spent in the queue since the last event occurred is equal to the current value for Number of Parts in the Queueing Buffer (NPIQ) multiplied by the time span since the last event (TSLE). The product is then added to the current value of CMPIQ.

$$CPMIQ=CPMIQ+(NPIQ \times TSLE)$$

4. Determine the Average Queue Length observed over the current time span. The Average Queue Length (AVGQL) is equal to the current value of CPMIQ divided by the current value of CLOCK. If CLOCK=0 then AVGQL=0.

If CLOCK>>0 then AVGQL=CPMIQ ÷ CLOCK else AVGQL=0

5. Go to the instructions for **Creating A Variable Status Report** on page 3-12.

Instructions For Creating A Variable Status Report

1. Record the current values from Table 3A for the specified variables (CLOCK, TPA, TPM, MACHST, NPIQ, MPIQ, AVGQL) displayed in Table 3B below. Each time these instructions are completed, another row of output data is produced.

2. End the simulation exercise or continue? If continue, go to task number three below. Otherwise, stop.

3. If the value of the variable ETYPE in Table 3A equals ARV (ETYPE=ARV) then go to the instructions for **Processing A Part Arrival Event** on page 3-13. If ETYPE=DEP, then go to the instructions for **Processing A Part Departure Event** on page 3-14.

Table 3B Variable Status Report

	CLOCK	TPA	TPM	MACHST	NPIQ	MPIQ	AVGQL
1	0	0	0	IDLE	0	0	0
2	3	1	0	BUSY	0	0	0
3	5	2	0	BUSY	1	1	0.40
4	6	2	1	BUSY	0	1	0.33
5	7	3	1	BUSY	1	1	0.43
6							
7							
8							
9							
10							

JMI Consulting Group © 1995

Processing A Part Arrival Event

1. Increment the value of the Total Parts Arrived (TPA) variable in Table 3A by one.
   TPA=TPA+1

2. Determine the time span between the current clock time and the time of the next part arrival. This is accomplished by rolling a single die. The resulting value represents the time in minutes before the next part arrival.
   Die Value = 1,2,3,4,5 or 6

3. In Table 3A, update the value of the variable Next Part Arrival Time (NPAT). This is achieved by adding the value of the die roll to the current simulation clock time (CLOCK). The new value for NPAT is recorded in Table 3A.
   NPAT=CLOCK+Die Value

The remaining tasks depend on the current state of the machine. Is it IDLE or BUSY? The following procedures are performed based on that answer:

4. DOES MACHST = IDLE?

☞⇦⇦YES⇦⇦↩   ↯⇨⇨NO⇨⇨↯

YES	NO
5. Set the value of the machine state variable in Table 3A equal to BUSY. **MACHST=BUSY**	5. Increment the value of the variable NPIQ in Table 3A by 1. **NPIQ=NPIQ+1**
6. Determine the time span between the current clock time and the time of the next part departure (cycle time of a part at the machine). This is accomplished by rolling a single die. The resulting value represents the time in minutes before the next part departure. **Die Value = 1,2,3,4,5 or 6**	6. Go to Table 3A. Check for maximum parts in queue. If the current number of parts in the queueing buffer (NPIQ) is greater than the current value for maximum number of parts observed in the queue (MPIQ), then replace the value for MPIQ with NPIQ. **If NPIQ>>MPIQ then MPIQ=NPIQ**
7. Update the Next Part Departure Time (NPDT) in Table 3A. This is achieved by adding the value of the die roll to the current simulation clock time (CLOCK). The new value for NPDT is recorded in Table 3A. **NPDT=CLOCK+Die Roll**	7. Go to the instructions for **Determining Next Event Types** on page 3-10.
8. Go to the instructions for **Determining Next Event Types** on page 3-10.	

Processing A Part Departure Event

1. Increment the value of the Total Parts Machined (TPM) variable in Table 3A by one.

TPM=TPM+1

The remaining tasks are dependent upon the number of parts in the queueing buffer (NPIQ). They involve updating the variable values for machine state (MACHST), Next Part Departure Time (NPDT) and Number of Parts In Queue (NPIQ). The procedures for performing these tasks are specified below.

2. IS THE QUEUEING BUFFER (NPIQ) EMPTY?

NPIQ = 0?

⇦⇦⇦YES⇦⇦⇦   ⇨⇨⇨NO⇨⇨⇨

3. Set the value of the machine state variable (MACHST) in Table 3A equal to IDLE.

MACHST=IDLE

4. Set the value of the Next Part Departure Time variable (NPDT) in Table 3A equal to None Scheduled (NS)

NPDT=NS

5. Go to the instructions for **Determining Next Event Types** on page 3-10.

3. Go to Table 3A. Decrease the current number of parts in the queueing buffer (NPIQ) by 1.

NPIQ=NPIQ-1

4. Determine the time span between the current clock time and the time of the next part departure (the cycle time of a part at the machine). This is accomplished by rolling a single die. The resulting value represents the time in minutes before the next part departure.

Die Value = 1,2,3,4,5 or 6

5. Update the Next Part Departure Time (NPDT) in Table 3A. This is achieved by adding the value of the die roll to the current simulation clock time (CLOCK). The new value for NPDT is recorded in Table 3A.

NPDT=CLOCK+Die Roll

6. Go to the instructions for **Determining Next Event Types** on page 3-10.

Chapter 4

SIMULATION TERMINOLOGY

STEPS TO LEARNING SIMULATION
1. What Is Simulation?
2. Why Simulate?
3. How Does Simulation Work?
4. Simulation Terminology
5. Simulation Products
6. Understanding Probability Distributions
7. Extracting Values From Probability Distributions
8. Finding A Distribution To Represent Data
9. Statistical Analyses Of Simulation Output
10. Building A Cost Perspective Into Simulation
11. Conducting A Successful Simulation Project
12. Avoiding Simulation Pitfalls
13. Where Can Simulation Be Used?
14. Assessing Savings From A Simulation Investment

Simulation Terminology

- System And System State

- Discrete And Continuous Events

- Static And Dynamic Models

- Stochastic And Deterministic Models

- Steady-State And Terminating Simulations

- Warm-up Period

- Model Verification And Validation

- Random Number Streams And Seeds

- Model Run And Independent Model Replication

System And System State

A <u>system</u> is an organized group of entities such as people, equipment, methods, principles, and parts which come together and work as a unit. A simulation model characterizes a system by mathematically describing the responses that can result from the interactions of a system's entities.

<u>System state</u> is the collection of variables, stochastic (can change randomly) and deterministic (not influenced by probability), which contain all the information necessary to describe a system at any point in time [Smith (1989)].

Discrete And Continuous Event Models

A <u>discrete event</u> is an instantaneous action that occurs at a unique point in time. An airplane landing at an airport, a part arriving at a delivery dock, a customer arriving at a bank, and a machine finishing a cycle are examples of discrete events. The occurrences of these events can cause system states to change.

A <u>continuous event</u> is an action without cessation. It continues uninterrupted with respect to time. The temperature of water in a lake rising and lowering during a day, the flowing of oil into a tanker, and chemical conversions are simple examples. Continuous events involve a time rate of change. They are usually represented by differential equations [e.g., $\frac{du}{dt} = -k(u-10)$ where $\frac{du}{dt}$ is the change of temperature with respect to time].

Static And Dynamic Models

A <u>static model</u> refers to a model that is not influenced by time. There is no simulation clock involved. Seconds, hours and days play no role in a model. The state of a model does not change with respect to time. A simulation model that imitates the roll of a die is an example. The output of the model, (1, 2, 3, 4, 5, or 6), is not affected by time.

A <u>dynamic model</u> is a model which is influenced by time. The state of the model evolves over simulated seconds, hours, days and months. A mathematical clock is used to track simulated time. Service and manufacturing related systems are generally represented with this type of model. WIP levels, production schedules, equipment utilizations, customer arrival rates, and throughput are a few examples of dynamic variables. Their values can change with respect to time.

Stochastic And Deterministic Models

A <u>stochastic model</u> contains processes controlled by random variables. The word **variable** implies that something is capable of changing. It does not have a specific value, but rather a range of values. **Random** signifies that the changes can occur with no particular pattern. A stochastic process is composed of a sequence of randomly determined values. Time between failures on a piece of equipment is an example of a stochastic process. The time required to repair the equipment is another. Time values for both can change indiscriminately with each occurrence.

A **deterministic model** is any model that does not contain random variables. Results produced by this type of model are not influenced by probability. An example is a model which solely utilizes average values or constants to represent the functions and characteristics of its entities. A spreadsheet analysis could be considered a deterministic model.

Steady-State And Terminating Simulations

A **steady-state** simulation implies that the system state is independent of its initial start-up conditions. Analyses from these models are based on output data generated after steady-state conditions are achieved. The cumulative average of multiple die rolls can be used to demonstrate this principle. After a certain number of rolls, the cumulative average of all values rolled will remain at approximately **3.5**. The point at which this occurs exemplifies a steady-state condition. This concept is further illustrated in Graph G4A. The cumulative moving average from **1000** rolls of a die are shown there. A steady-state condition for the average value of a die roll occurs approximately after the 500th roll.

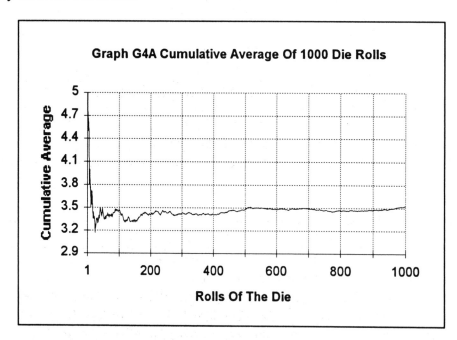

A **terminating simulation** runs for a predetermined length of time or until a specific event occurs. Analyses and conclusions are based on output values produced at the stopping point. The results of terminating simulations are usually dependent upon the initial values and quantities used when starting the model. For this reason, **the start-up conditions in terminating models should**

accurately reflect the start-up circumstances exhibited in the real world system that is being studied.

The decision to employ a steady-state or terminating simulation is made during the preliminary planning stages of a simulation project. The choice is dependent upon the type of system being modeled. A facility which manufactures bottles twenty-four hours per day would likely be analyzed with a steady-state simulation. For other types of systems, this may not be applicable.

Many real world systems may never reach a steady-state condition. Consider an automated storage/retrieval system consisting of six independently functioning carrousels. The carrousels contain tote-pans which house parts for a production process. Each carrousel is subjected to random storage/retrieval requests for parts during production hours. All totes are returned to the carrousels at the end of each production shift, such that each carrousel begins a new shift with zero storage/retrieval requests.

Suppose the objective of a simulation study is to determine the average wait time an order request experiences at a carrousel during a single production shift. Steady-state conditions for order queue lengths may not occur during this time duration. Given these circumstances, a terminating simulation would probably be used to analyze the system.

Warm-up Period

A **warm-up period** is the amount of time that a model needs to run before statistical data collection begins. The length of the period is dependent upon the type of model being used; terminating or steady-state. Warm-up periods for the latter can be found through experimentation with moving averages. A terminating model may utilize a warm-up period equal to the time required for the model to achieve a system state equivalent to pre-determined starting conditions. The starting conditions represent the initial state of the system being studied (e.g., Machine A begins the simulation with ten parts queued in front of it, Machine B has thirty, and so forth).

Model Verification And Validation

Model verification is a simulation term that implies that a model is operating in its intended manner. Consider a simple system consisting of a conveyor feeding parts to a machine. A simulation model is developed to analyze parts queueing on the conveyor. The model can be deemed verified when it reflects the following conditions: 1) parts arrive at the conveyor per a desired rate, 2) parts are serviced at the machine per a desired rate, and 3) parts queueing on the conveyor are being counted correctly.

Model validation implies that the results generated by a model coincide with the results produced by the system being represented by the model. Consider a manufacturing system which is known to have an average product makespan (total time required to manufacture a product) of 22 days.

Suppose a model of that system is subjected to the same conditions experienced in the real-world system, and the results generated by it indicate an average product makespan reasonably close to 22 days. The model can probably be considered validated if product makespan is the sole factor being studied. **A validated model opens the door to what-if analyses**.

Sometimes simulation is used to analyze theoretical systems which do not physically exist. Model validation is not possible prior to hypothesis testing. In these cases, model builders must rely on system experts to establish the reasonableness of the results. Model verification becomes a major element for establishing rational validity.

Random Number Streams And Seeds

A **random number stream** is a sequence of random numbers where each succeeding number is calculated from the previous number derived. The initial number is referred to as the **random number seed**. Random numbers with values between zero and one play an important role in extracting values from probability distributions. Probability distributions are the bases for generating stochastic behavior (random variates) in simulations. More information on this subject is presented in chapter 7, *"Extracting Values From Probability Distributions."*

Model Run And Independent Model Replication

A **model run** involves operating a simulation for a specified period of time with a unique set of random values. An **independent model replication** entails operating the same model for the same period of time with a different set of random values. Multiple model replications are always required when analyzing results from stochastic simulations. **It is vital to recognize the following: Results from a single model replication of a stochastic simulation are themselves stochastic**.

The following example illustrates the concept of an independent model replication. Picture a bag containing **100** ping-pong balls, each marked with a unique number. Suppose someone reaches into the bag and extracts one ball. The number on the ball is **35**. A conclusion that all balls in the bag are marked with the number **35** should obviously not be made. The results of an independent model replication are representative of a single ping-pong ball in the bag. Chapter 9, *"Statistical Analyses Of Simulation Output,"* discusses this subject in greater detail.

Chapter 5

SIMULATION PRODUCTS

Simulation Products

- What Is A Simulation Language?

- What Is A Simulator?

- What Questions Should Be Asked When Selecting A Simulation Package?

  ◊ What are our current and future simulation applications?

  ◊ What level of detail will be required in the models?

  ◊ What type of time constraints will there be on project durations?

  ◊ Who will be building the models and how will the end-users utilize them?

  ◊ Do model size limitations need to be considered?

  ◊ What environments will a package operate in?

  ◊ What are the statistical capabilities of the package?

  ◊ Does the package have global attribute features?

  ◊ Can data be imported from and exported to external data files?

  ◊ Can multiple model runs be made without human intervention between runs?

What Is A Simulation Language?

A **computer language** is a system of words and commands that are used to instruct a computer to perform a specific task. Programming is the actual writing of the words and commands. **Simulation languages** are computer languages that instruct computers to process information in a manner that will imitate a system's operation.

FORTRAN was a programming language used extensively with simulation in the late 1950's. Models were developed by writing instructions in terms of the FORTRAN language. Programming (code writing) was required for every aspect of a model.

Most of today's simulation languages are classified as **general purpose languages**. They contain previously written programming statements or modules for modeling generic elements (e.g., queues, random number generators, probability distributions). Model building is much faster with these languages when compared to standard programming languages like FORTRAN or C.

A simulation language can be used to model almost any kind of system. They are not limited by specific application areas, or model size. A potential disadvantage is the amount of programming expertise required to use them. It tends to be greater with simulation languages as compared to simulators. Those who have prior programming experience are more likely to master a simulation language faster than those who do not have previous experience.

What Is A Simulator?

Simulators are software packages that focus on specific application areas. They generally require minimal programming skills. A model is developed by describing a real system's elements and dynamics in terms of predefined elements contained within a simulator. Menu-driven input screens often prompt the model builder for specific information as he or she is constructing a model.

One of the main advantages of simulators is their ability to quickly construct models in the absence of programming expertise. Operational personnel usually find them easier to understand, and to work with. A possible drawback is their limited capacity to model systems outside their specific application areas. Modeling complex logics can also be difficult. However, many simulators have reduced the magnitude of the latter by providing basic commands such as If-Then-Else, for addressing more intricate logic. Others also provide a simulation language interface for modeling components that are not describable in terms of a simulator's predefined elements.

The difference between simulation languages and simulators is diminishing. Simulator based packages are striving to provide more language based features and language based packages are striving to provide more simulator features. A primary goal of most simulation software manufacturers is to make simulation easier for the user. They have, and are continuing to do an excellent job in accomplishing that goal.

What Are Some Of The Simulation Packages That Are Available Today?

Simulation technology and products are constantly changing. The Society For Computer Simulation International (SCS) provides an annual publication that contains comparative information regarding the majority of simulation products. It categorizes them by their application areas, cost, and other product specific information. Vendor addresses and telephone numbers are also included. The publication can be purchased for approximately forty dollars. The address for the SCS is P.O. Box 17900, San Diego, CA 92177, Phone: 619-277-3888, Fax: 619-277-3930 and Email scs@sdsc.edu.

The selection of a simulation package should be based on the specific needs of a user. Finding a package that will ultimately satisfy your requirements is best accomplished by experimenting with multiple packages to investigate their individual qualifications. Most simulation vendors provide a means for evaluating their products prior to purchasing them.

What Questions Should Be Asked When Selecting A Simulation Package?

What are our current and future simulation applications?
One of the first questions that must be addressed prior to selecting a simulation package is, "What are our current and future simulation applications?" A package's modeling range should be as flexible as the diversity of the potential application areas. If the applications are solely manufacturing related, then a package that caters specifically to manufacturing operations would probably be advantageous over one that supports communications, chemical processing, and other domains. If a large variety of systems will be modeled, then a package that accommodates a broad array is likely a better choice.

What level of detail will be required in the models?
The level of detail anticipated in models should correspond directly with the detailing capacity of a simulation package. Suppose simulation is to be used for modeling complex control logic in large scale conveyor systems, or complicated conditional labor allocation within a manufacturing operation. These types of applications may require a package that provides intricate detailing capabilities.

Continuous event modeling may be necessary or advantageous in some applications. Industries such as food or chemical processing often require this feature. Elements that involve rates of flow are candidates for continuous event modeling. Sometimes a combination of both discrete and continuous event is needed. Many packages do not possess both features.

What type of time constraints will there be on project durations?

Projects subject to time constraints, such as short completion schedules, would likely need a simulation package that features rapid model building capabilities. Building models rapidly requires good debugging features, effective communication abilities, and fast model execution speeds. The effort required to interact with a model and to make changes to it should also be assessed.

Who will be building the models and how will the end users utilize them?

A learning-curve factor is another issue that should be addressed when selecting a package. How much time is required to become proficient with a package's model building features? Model builders with limited or no programming background will probably be more comfortable with a package that minimizes code writing activities. The same applies for the end users of a model. Perhaps a model will be used as a dynamic tool for evaluating future alternatives. The end users must be able to readily interact with a model, incorporate changes into it, and interpret and understand the results.

Documentation, training, and customer support provided with a package should also be evaluated. Each of these factors can influence the learning curve for a model builder to become productive with a package.

Do model size limitations need to be considered?

The size of a model grows as elements and detail are added to it. A system containing many elements and interrelationships may require a large model to represent it. Some PC based simulators may limit the size of their models. The number of elements permitted in a model is sometimes fixed. For example, a manufacturing simulator may have a limited number of machines or labor types which are available for constructing a model. (Model sizes for both language based packages and simulators will ultimately be limited by the capacity of the hardware on which they are operating).

Model size can impact model execution time. Large models will typically have longer execution times. Model execution time is also affected by the hardware being used, and the manner in which a model is constructed (e.g., effective use of the software package's modeling features). Testing several alternatives can necessitate numerous model runs and replications. It is desirable to have the ratio of actual run time to simulation time as small as possible. Large models can produce ratios considerably greater than one. Eight hours of computer time to produce eight hours of simulated time would not be advantageous when many replications are required. Sometimes the hardware can be changed to improve the execution time. This issue is discussed in the following subject.

What environments can a package operate in?

The operating environments (PC, Macintosh, workstations, mini-computers, and mainframes) vary for different packages. Some will work in only one environment, whereas others will operate on multiple platforms. A mini-computer, workstations on a Local Area Network (LAN), or mainframe environment may be advantageous when there will be multiple users of a simulation package. It can also be cost effective to build and verify models in a PC environment and then make the model replications on a platform that can provide faster model execution times. In many cases, a PC environment may be the fastest choice (e.g., in a mainframe environment, a simulation job main be competing for processing time with several other jobs on the system).

What are the statistical capabilities of a package?

Statistical capabilities can be viewed from two perspectives. One involves a package's ability to collect statistical data during model runs in conjunction with its capacity to analyze and communicate the results. The effort required to produce histograms, time-series graphs, statistical analyses and other output reports vary with each simulation package. Batch modes, warm-up periods, methods for changing random number streams, and the ability to save results should be assessed.

A second consideration pertains to standard probability distributions. What standard distributions are provided with a package, and what effort is required to find standard distributions representative of empirical data? Random behavior is usually modeled through the employment of probability distributions. The number of standard distributions (continuous and discrete) provided with various packages can differ significantly. A good selection of distributions is essential when many stochastic processes are being modeled. The quantity of random number streams, and the effort needed to change them also contribute to a package's ability to represent stochastic behavior. It is usually desirable to have at least one hundred random number streams. The ease of changing streams and using their antithetic values should also be considered (see page 11.11-7, "What Are Antithetic Variates?").

Finding standard distributions representative of empirical data can be a tedious chore when done manually. Some packages offer features that will facilitate this task. Others have the ability to create user defined distributions from collected data. Both can reduce the model building effort.

Does the software package have global attribute features?

Attributes are a modeling feature that allow an object to be associated with something, while serving to identify something else. They can significantly enhance a package's model building capacity by providing a means for describing the characteristics and qualities of a system's entities. For example, a simulation entity may represent a television, and attributes associated with that television might be model number, screen size, and color.

Parts are a typical entity found in the majority of models pertaining to manufacturing systems. Attributes such as lot size, part description, or cycle time at an operation can be attached to individual parts. They remain with a part as it flows through a model. It is desirable to be able to change attribute values at any point within a model.

Can data be imported from, and exported to external data files?

Input data needed for simulation analyses is sometimes extracted from large databases. Product scheduling information from an MRP database is an example. It can be beneficial to be able to down-load this type of information to an external data file which can then be used within a model. It is also useful to be able to write simulation output to external files. These files can then be analyzed with other software packages. This is especially true for simulation packages that do not contain features for performing statistical analyses.

Can multiple model runs be made without human intervention between runs?

Performing multiple model replications can be very time consuming. When this occurs, it can be advantageous to make the replications during non-working hours (This is particularly beneficial for PC-based packages). Model replications for each scenario can be made and the results saved without human intervention between runs. Some packages contain features for accomplishing this and others do not. It should be considered when large models and lengthy runtimes are anticipated.

Simulation Of A Blank Page

Chapter 6

UNDERSTANDING PROBABILITY DISTRIBUTIONS

Understanding Probability Distributions

- What Are Probability Distributions And How Are They Used In Simulation Models?

- How Are Probability Distributions Created?

- What Is A Random Variable?

- What Is A Probability Density Function?

- Discrete And Continuous Probability Distributions?

- Means, Variances And Standard Deviations

What Are Probability Distributions And How Are They Used In Simulation Models?

A **probability distribution** is a set of values or measurements that relate the relative frequency with which an event occurs or is likely to occur. Stochastic simulation models utilize probability distributions to represent a multitude of random occurring events. Classical examples within the manufacturing sector are times between failures on a piece of equipment, and the times required to repair it. Interarrival times of customers into a system, occurrences of defects, and the cycle times associated with new or undefined tasks are some other examples. **In general, any process that repetitively produces outcomes that vary per iteration can usually be represented by a probability distribution**.

How Are Probability Distributions Created?

The first step in creating a probability distribution is to obtain empirical data (sometimes referred to as raw data). **Empirical data** is recorded information, whether it be counts or measurements, collected in its original form. The data in Table T6A is an example of raw data. It represents one hundred observations of time between arrivals of patients at a hospital.

Table T6A									
Time Between Arrivals of 100 Patients At A Hospital									
(All Times In Minutes)									
18	13	3	40	9	29	10	3	8	10
1	17	29	2	22	1	22	1	4	32
20	5	8	6	10	3	1	11	13	2
15	8	1	23	29	9	34	17	10	4
15	2	1	1	40	8	6	6	8	1
3	24	14	24	8	14	28	12	18	7
1	5	6	10	54	12	13	1	22	45
5	12	2	14	12	1	33	23	7	5
12	5	46	18	2	2	6	2	39	7
4	4	2	19	1	5	12	3	5	1

The second step involves creating a **relative frequency (probability) histogram** of the data. This is accomplished by grouping the data into intervals or cells. The number of intervals is usually between five and twenty, depending on the amount of data collected. With less data, fewer intervals are required. Table T6B on page 6-5 displays ten class intervals selected for the data in Table T6A. The frequency field reflects the quantity of data points that fall into each respective interval. <u>The relative frequency or probability is calculated by dividing the frequency number by the total number of data records.</u> It simply relates the percentage of all data points found in each interval. Graph G6A is a **probability histogram** for the data in Table T6B. It graphically displays the distribution of the data across all intervals.

What Is A Random Variable?

A <u>random variable</u> is a variable whose outcome is determined by the result of an experiment. The amount of time between arrivals at the receiving dock in the previous example can be considered a random variable. It changes indiscriminately over time. The range of possible values determines whether a random variable is **discrete** (finite possibilities), or **continuous** (infinite possibilities). A random variable is often designated by an upper case **X**, and the values associated with it are designated by a lower case **x**. If **X** is a random variable representing an interarrival time at a hospital, then **P(X ≤ x)** indicates the probability of the random variable **X** being less than or equal to a value **x**.

What Is A Probability Density Function?

A <u>probability density function</u> relates the probabilities corresponding to individual **x** values associated with a random variable **X**. (A probability histogram associates probabilities with groups of **x** values). Functions match pairs of numbers which are described by a mathematical equation. They can be expressed graphically by plotting the paired values. A horizontal axis typically signifies **x** values and a vertical axis usually denotes **y** values. The **y** values of a probability density function associate probabilities linked with individual values of **x**. It is for this reason that a probability density function is usually denoted as **y=f(x)** (interpreted as **y** is a function of **x**).

The mathematical equation that describes a density function is often difficult to establish. It can frequently be approximated by finding a known **standard probability distribution** (e.g., normal, exponential, gamma, etc.) which accurately represents the relative frequency distribution of the actual data. **The shape of a relative frequency histogram provides clues for finding a standard distribution representative of it**. For example, the shape of the histogram in Graph G6A on page 6-5 indicates an exponential distribution as a likely candidate to represent the probability distribution of the observed data. An exponential distribution has a probability density function which is mathematically represented as follows:

$$y = f(x) = \frac{1}{\beta}\, e^{-x/\beta}$$

β (beta) is a scale parameter for the distribution. The value for β in an exponential distribution is equal to the distribution's mean.

Table T6B
Relative Frequency Of Interarrival Times

Class Interval	Frequency	Probability	
0-5	36	$\frac{36}{100}$	0.36
6-10	21	$\frac{21}{100}$	0.21
11-15	15	$\frac{15}{100}$	0.15
16-20	7	$\frac{7}{100}$	0.07
21-25	8	$\frac{8}{100}$	0.08
26-30	4	$\frac{4}{100}$	0.04
31-35	3	$\frac{3}{100}$	0.03
36-40	3	$\frac{3}{100}$	0.03
41-45	1	$\frac{1}{100}$	0.01
46-50	1	$\frac{1}{100}$	0.01
>50	1	$\frac{1}{100}$	0.01

Total Quantity of Data Samples = 100

Graph G6A

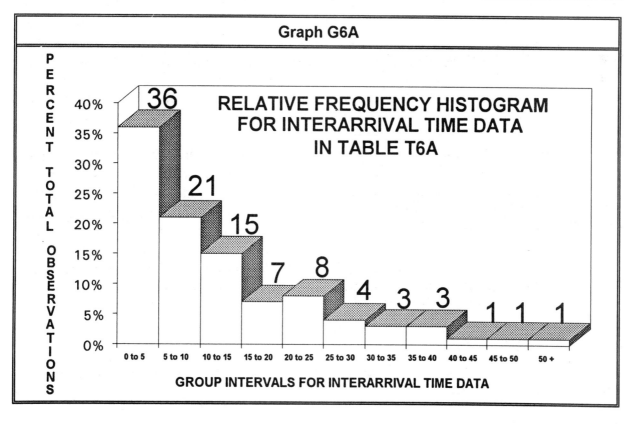

RELATIVE FREQUENCY HISTOGRAM FOR INTERARRIVAL TIME DATA IN TABLE T6A

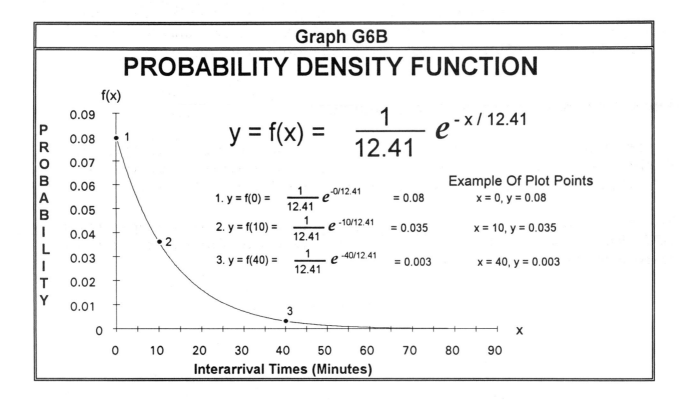

Graph G6B

PROBABILITY DENSITY FUNCTION

$$y = f(x) = \frac{1}{12.41} e^{-x/12.41}$$

Example Of Plot Points

1. $y = f(0) = \dfrac{1}{12.41} e^{-0/12.41} = 0.08$ x = 0, y = 0.08

2. $y = f(10) = \dfrac{1}{12.41} e^{-10/12.41} = 0.035$ x = 10, y = 0.035

3. $y = f(40) = \dfrac{1}{12.41} e^{-40/12.41} = 0.003$ x = 40, y = 0.003

Interarrival Times (Minutes)

The calculated average for the interarrival time data in Table T6A is 12.41 minutes. Graph G6B displays an exponential distribution with a β parameter equal to 12.41. This distribution is hypothesized as being a good portrayal for the interarrival time data. (The chapter, *"Finding A Distribution To Represent Data,"* provides additional information on how to verify a fit between an empirical probability distribution and a standard probability distribution).

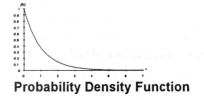

Probability Density Function

The shape of the exponential distribution is similar to the histogram shape

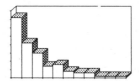

Relative Frequency Histogram

Discrete And Continuous Probability Distributions

A **discrete probability distribution** is a distribution with a finite number of **x** values. A probability distribution associated with the rolling of a die is an example of this type of distribution. There are only six unique **x** values associated with a die **1**, **2**, **3**, **4**, **5**, and **6**.

A **continuous probability distribution** is a distribution which contains an infinite number of **x** values. If the number of possible **x** values equal the number of points on a line segment, then the distribution is continuous. Consider a continuous uniform probability distribution (the probability for any given value is the same) with values ranging from **1** to **6**. Some values from this distribution are **1.1**, **1.134**, **2.456**, **2.56**, **3.345**, and **4.897**. The number of possibilities is infinite.

Means, Variances And Standard Deviations

A **mean** is the average. An estimate of a mean is obtained by adding quantities together and dividing the sum by the total number of quantities. Suppose we have ten values as follows: **1, 2, 4, 4, 5, 7, 7, 8, 9,** and **10**. The mean is **(1+2+4+4+5+7+7+8+9+10)** divided by **10**, or **5.7**.

The mean of a probability distribution can be thought of in terms of mass. The mass represents the density locations of the probability. The mean value is the point at which the distribution will balance itself when placed on a support point.

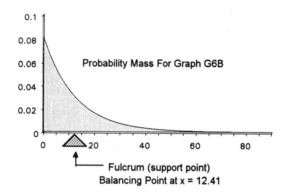

The **variance of a probability distribution** measures the degree of change between the random variable values and the mean of the distribution. **Standard deviation** is the square root of the variance. If the variance of a distribution equals **36**, then the standard deviation equals the square root of **36** (designated as $\sqrt{36}$). The $\sqrt{36}$ is equal to **6**. The chapter, "*Statistical Analyses Of Simulation Output*," further defines the mathematical equations for estimating the means and variances of probability distributions.

Simulation Of A Blank Page

Chapter 7

EXTRACTING VALUES FROM PROBABILITY DISTRIBUTIONS

Extracting Values From Probability Distributions

- What Is A Cumulative Probability Distribution?

- What Is A Cumulative Distribution Function?

- What Is A Random Number?

- What Is A Random Number Generator?

- How Are Random Numbers Used To Extract Values From Probability Distributions?

What Is A Cumulative Probability Distribution?

A **cumulative probability distribution** reveals the percentage of all occurrences that will have a value less than or equal to a given random variable value. It is derived through the successive totaling of probabilities associated with each possible value for a random variable. The final sum should always be equal to one. The roll of a die can be used to illustrate this principle. There are six random variable values associated with the roll of a die. They are **1, 2, 3, 4, 5** and **6**. The probability of occurrence for any given value is **1/6**. The odds of rolling a value less than or equal to two, three, four, five, or six are respectively **2/6**, **3/6**, **4/6**, **5/6**, and **1**.

Table T7A demonstrates the derivation of a cumulative probability distribution for the data presented in Table T6A on page 6-3. It tells us the likelihood of an interarrival time being less than or equal to any given time. For example, we can expect an average of seventy-nine out of every one hundred interarrival times to be less than or equal to twenty minutes.

Table T7A Cumulative Probability			
Class Interval	**Frequency**	**Probability**	**Cumulative Probability**
0-5	36	0.36	0.36
6-10	21	0.21	0.36+0.21 = 0.57
11-15	15	0.15	0.36+0.21+0.15 = 0.72
16-20	7	0.07	0.36+0.21+0.15+0.07 = 0.79
21-25	8	0.08	0.36+0.21+0.15+0.07+0.08 = 0.87
26-30	4	0.04	0.36+0.21+0.15+0.07+0.08+0.04 = 0.91
31-35	3	0.03	0.36+0.21+0.15+0.07+0.08+0.04+0.03 = 0.94
36-40	3	0.03	0.36+0.21+0.15+0.07+0.08+0.04+0.03+0.03 = 0.97
41-45	1	0.01	0.36+0.21+0.15+0.07+0.08+0.04+0.03+0.03+0.01 = 0.98
46-50	1	0.01	0.36+0.21+0.15+0.07+0.08+0.04+0.03+0.03+0.01+0.01 = 0.99
>50	1	0.01	0.36+0.21+0.15+0.07+0.08+0.04+0.03+0.03+0.01+0.01 +0.01 = 1.00

What Is A Cumulative Distribution Function?

A **cumulative distribution function** mathematically describes the relationship between the values associated with a random variable and their cumulative probabilities. Like a density function, it matches pairs of values. The **y-axis** denotes cumulative probabilities and the **x-axis** designates the range of values for a random variable. The equation of the line created by the matched **(x,y)** points can be determined from the probability density function. In terms of calculus, the cumulative distribution function is obtained by integrating the probability density function $\int f(x)dx$ over the range of all possible values for **x**. Graph G7A depicts a cumulative probability function for the density function displayed in Graph G6B.

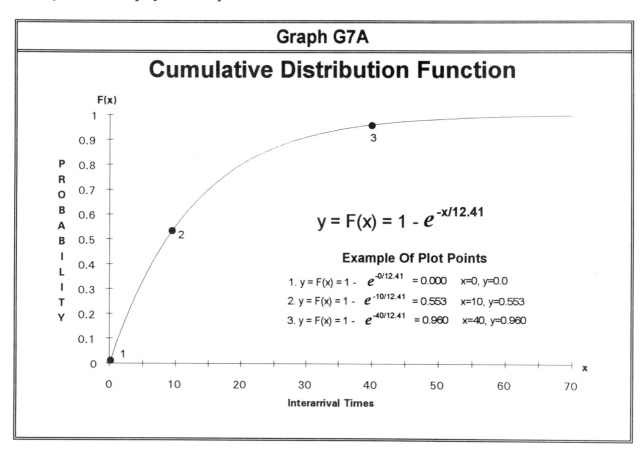

Graph G7A

Cumulative Distribution Function

$$y = F(x) = 1 - e^{-x/12.41}$$

Example Of Plot Points

1. $y = F(x) = 1 - e^{-0/12.41} = 0.000$ x=0, y=0.0
2. $y = F(x) = 1 - e^{-10/12.41} = 0.553$ x=10, y=0.553
3. $y = F(x) = 1 - e^{-40/12.41} = 0.960$ x=40, y=0.960

Interarrival Times

What Is A Random Number?

A **random number** is any number that is obtained in a manner which has no particular pattern, purpose or reason. A simple example using ping-pong balls can illustrate this definition. Ten ping-pong balls are marked with the numbers zero through nine. The balls are all placed in a paper bag. Someone indiscriminately reaches into the bag and removes one ball. The number on the ball selected is a random number. Random numbers with values between zero and one play a major role in establishing stochastic behavior in simulation models.

What Is A Random Number Generator?

A **random number generator** is any mechanism that produces independent random numbers. The term "independent" implies that the probability of producing any given random number remains the same each time a number is produced. If the extracted ping-pong ball in the previous sub-topic (*What is a Random Number*) is always returned to the bag prior to the next extraction, then each random number produced is independent.

Random number generators produce a sequence of random numbers. Each new number is calculated from the previously computed number. The initial number is referred to as the **number seed**, and the sequence of numbers generated from it is called a **random number stream**. By definition, a true random number can not be predicted. Numbers produced by a random number generator are calculated, and a calculated number is predictable. Therefore, the numbers created by a random number generator are often referred to as pseudo (having a deceptive resemblance) random numbers.

A **linear congruent generator** is one of the most common generators used to produce decimal (values between **0** and **1**) random numbers. It generates a sequence of random numbers through the use of a mathematical technique called remainder division. The result of this technique is the integer value remaining after a division operation is performed. For example, **10 MOD 6** is interpreted as the whole-integer remainder of **10** divided by **6**, which is equal to **4**. The number **6** is the modulus in this particular example.

Table 7B Output From Linear Congruent Generator

$$x_{n+1} = (ax_n + c) \text{ MOD } m \qquad R_{n+1} = \frac{x_{n+1}}{m} \qquad x_0=7, a=9, c=1, m=17$$

n	x_n	$9x_n + 1$		$(9x_n + 1) \text{ MOD } 17$ x_{n+1}		$x_{n+1} \div 17$ R_{n+1}	
0	$x_0=7$	$(9 \times 7) + 1 =$	64	$64 \text{ MOD } 17 =$	$x_1=13$	$\frac{13}{17} =$	0.7647
1	$x_1=13$	$(9 \times 13) + 1 =$	118	$118 \text{ MOD } 17 =$	$x_2=16$	$\frac{16}{17} =$	0.9412
2	$x_2=16$		145		$x_3=9$		0.5294
3	$x_3=9$		82		$x_4=14$		0.8235
4	$x_4=14$		127		$x_5=8$		0.4706
5	$x_5=8$		73		$x_6=5$		0.2941
6	$x_6=5$		46		$x_7=12$		0.7059
7	$x_7=12$		109		$x_8=7$		0.4118
8	$x_8=7$		64		$x_9=13$		0.7647
9	$x_9=13$		118		$x_{10}=16$		0.9412
10	$x_{10}=16$		145		$x_{11}=9$		0.5294

The basic algorithm for a linear congruent generator is $x_{n+1} = (ax_n + c)$ MOD m, where x_{n+1} is the n-th remainder value after the n-th modulus operation. X_0 is referred to as the random number seed (Initial number from which a sequence of numbers is produced). R_{n+1} is the n-th pseudo decimal random number produced. It is obtained by dividing the value of x_{n+1} by the modulus m. Table T7B (page 7-5) illustrates the results of this algorithm for a=9, c=1, m=17 and x_0= 7. The selections of the values for a, c, and m determine the frequency (the point at which the generated numbers begin to repeat) for a random number stream. The stream in this example has a frequency of eight numbers.

It is desirable to have random number streams which have a frequency of one hundred thousand or more when many stochastic processes (processes containing random occurring events) are being modeled. One such generator that accomplishes this is Marse and Roberts' portable random number generator UNIRAN [Marse and Roberts (1983) (see Appendix B, page B8)]. The values for a, m and c are a=630,360,016, m=2^{32-1} and c=0. Two random number streams are generated from that algorithm. Table T7C (page 7-7) displays the first ten numbers in each stream.

How Are Random Numbers Used To Extract Values From Probability Distributions?

The fundamental logic used for extracting random values from probability distributions is based on a cumulative distribution function and a random number generator. The cumulative distribution function has y values that range between zero and one. Random number generators, as described earlier, produce a set of numbers which are uniformly distributed across this interval. For every y value (decimal number with a value between zero and one) a unique x value (random variate value) can be calculated.

Let's assume that the interarrival time data in Table T6A in chapter 6, "*Understanding Probability Distributions*," can be accurately represented by the probability density function $y = f(x) = (1/12.41) e^{-x/12.41}$. The mathematical equation for the cumulative distribution function is $y = F(x) = 1 - e^{-x/12.41}$. For this particular function, x values (interarrival times) can be calculated according to the following equation: $x = \ln(1 - y)(-12.41)$ where y is a decimal random number produced by a random number generator, and $\ln(1 - y)$ is the natural logarithm of $1 - y$. Table T7D (page 7-7) applies this equation to the random number streams exhibited in Table T7C. Notice that a different sequence of interarrival times is produced by each stream. Suppose a thousand interarrival times are produced by each stream and a relative frequency histogram is made for each set of times. Both histograms will look similar to the following:

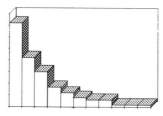

Table T7C Random Number Streams

Random Number Stream #1 Seed# 281629770	Random Number Stream #2 Seed# 539712780
0.18875	0.68427
0.25944	0.34968
0.57801	0.15477
0.64548	0.37851
0.25430	0.57164
0.85714	0.97741
0.96523	0.19258
0.66868	0.16903
0.24658	0.88034
0.14217	0.54566

Table T7D Random Interarrival Times

Random Number Stream #1		Random Number Stream #2	
y values	Interarrival Times x = ln(1-y)(-12.41)	y values	Interarrival Times x = ln(1-y)(-12.41)
0.18875	2.60	0.68427	14.31
0.25944	3.73	0.34968	5.34
0.57801	10.71	0.15477	2.09
0.64548	12.87	0.37851	5.90
0.25430	3.49	0.57164	10.52
0.85714	24.14	0.97741	47.04
0.96523	41.69	0.19258	2.65
0.66868	13.71	0.16903	2.30
0.24658	3.51	0.88034	26.35
0.14217	1.90	0.54566	9.79

The previously described method for generating random variates is referred to as the **inverse-transformation method**. It demonstrates how mathematics can be used to extract values from a probability distribution. Other methods, such as, composition and acceptance-rejection, are also used for this task [see Pritsker (1986) pages 708-710]. Simulation applies these mathematical methods to imitate stochastic behavior in a real or hypothesized system.

It is important to emphasize the following: Today's simulation packages do not require a model builder to write coding for generating random number streams or for performing inverse-transformations. The coding is already contained within statements or elements provided by a package. Generally, a model builder simply 1) selects a probability distribution from which he or she desires random variates, 2) specifies the input parameters for the distribution (see chapter "*Finding A Distribution To Represent Data*") and 3) designates a random number stream to be used with the distribution.

Chapter 8

FINDING A DISTRIBUTION TO REPRESENT DATA

Finding A Distribution To Represent Data

- What Are Some Of The Standard Probability Distributions Used With Simulation Modeling?

- Why Are Standard Distributions Used To Represent Empirical Data?

- What Is A Chi-Square "Goodness-Of-Fit" Test

- How Is A Chi-Square "Goodness-Of-Fit" Test Performed?

What Are Some Of The Standard Probability Distributions Used With Simulation Modeling?

Standard probability distributions are usually perceived in terms of the forms produced by their probability density functions. For example, the bell shaped curve is the figure typically associated with a normal distribution. Many probability density functions have parameters which control their shape and scale characteristics. Two of the more common are the α (alpha) parameter (determines the shape of a distribution) and the β (beta) parameter (determines the scale values in the range of a distribution). The means and variances of these distributions are defined in terms of the α and β parameters.

There are several standard continuous probability distributions that are frequently used with simulation. Some of these are the **Exponential, Gamma, Normal, Uniform, Weibull, Triangular, Lognormal, Erlang,** and **Beta** distributions. Appendix B contains additional properties associated with each distribution.

Standard probability distributions are used to represent empirical data distributions. The use of one standard distribution over another is totally dependent upon the empirical data which it is representing, or the type of stochastic process which is being modeled (when no data is available). A method for finding a standard distribution which is representative of empirical data is discussed at the end of this chapter.

Understanding the key characteristics and typical uses for standard probability distributions can help model builders find representative distributions for empirical data, and for processes where no historical data exists. Some of the more common uses for the previously mentioned standard probability distributions are as follows:

EXPONENTIAL
$$f(x) = \frac{1}{\beta} e^{-x/\beta}$$

Sometimes this distribution is referred to as the **Negative Exponential** distribution. It has widespread use in queueing systems. It is utilized to generate random values for the time between arrivals of customers into a system. The term "customers" covers an infinite number of possibilities ranging from packages arriving at a delivery dock to job requests on a computer system. Other possible applications for the negative exponetial distribution are: 1) the time to complete a task and 2) the time until failure for an electronic component.

Typical Specification Parameters: Mean value β, and Random Number Stream

GAMMA
$$f(x) = \frac{\beta^{-\alpha} x^{\alpha-1} e^{-x/\beta}}{\Gamma(\alpha)}$$

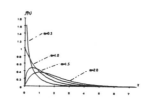

The gamma distribution is defined in terms of an α and β parameter. When $\alpha=1$, it becomes an exponential distribution. This distribution can be used to represent the time needed to complete a task or group of tasks. Suppose an exponential distribution with a mean parameter of $\beta = 1.2$ hours describes the time to complete a given task. The gamma distribution could be employed to generate values representing the total time required to complete n independent performances of that task. The α value would equal n for this scenario.

Typical Specification Parameters: α value, β value, and Random Number Stream

NORMAL
$$f(x) = \frac{1}{\sqrt{2\pi\sigma^2}} e^{-(x-\mu)^2/2\sigma^2}$$

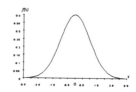

The normal distribution is often utilized to measure various types of error. Receiving/inspection operations frequently require the use of calibrated instruments to measure the dimensions of various components. The measurements revealed by an instrument are assumed to be normally distributed about the true dimensions of the component. A normal distribution could be used to represent the readings obtained on each individual measurement.

Typical Specification Parameters: mean value μ, standard deviation value σ, and Random Number Stream

UNIFORM
$$f(x) = \frac{1}{b-a}$$

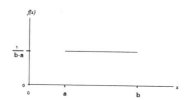

A uniform distribution over the range of zero to one is the basis for generating values from standard probability distributions. It can also be utilized to generate random values from customized algorithms. Another common application is to represent the time duration of a task when minimal information is known about the task. Sometimes the time to complete a task is believed to vary randomly and evenly between two values, **a** and **b**. Given these conditions, the uniform distribution is a good preliminary estimation for the cycle time duration.

Typical Specification Parameters: Minimum value **a**, Maximum value **b**, and Random Number Stream

WEIBULL $$f(x) = \alpha\beta^{-\alpha}x^{\alpha-1}e^{-(x/\beta)^\alpha}$$

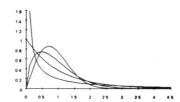

Reliability issues are often represented with a Weibull distribution. It can be used to generate values for the time to failure on a piece of equipment or the average life of an electronic component. The time to complete a task can also be reflected by this distribution.

Typical Specification Parameters: α value, β value, and Random Number Stream

TRIANGULAR

$$f(x) = \frac{2(x-a)}{(b-a)(c-a)} \quad \text{for } a \le x \le c$$

$$f(x) = \frac{2(b-x)}{(b-a)(b-c)} \quad \text{for } c \le x \le b$$

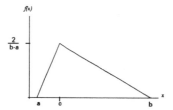

The triangular distribution is particularly useful for situations where only three pieces of information are known about a task. Ask assemblers on a production line how long it takes to perform an operation. Their response will likely be, "Most of the time it is this, but it ranges between this and that." The "this" (**a** value), "that" (**b** value), and "most of the time" (**c** value) can be used as the parameters of a triangular distribution.

Typical Specification Parameters: Minimum value **a**, Maximum value **b**, Mode value **c**, and Random Number Stream

LOGNORMAL

$$f(x) = \frac{1}{x\sqrt{2\pi\sigma^2}}\, e^{-(\ln x - \mu)^2/2\sigma^2}$$

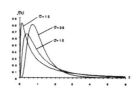

A lognormal distribution can be used to represent the time to perform a task. An example might be the cycle time for completing a carrousel storage/retrieval operation in an automated stores system. The parameter values for this distribution are generally calculated from the natural logarithms of the empirical data. Given these conditions, values generated from a lognormal distribution might be expressed in terms of the natural logarithms of the desired random values. If this is true, then the generated values must be converted to **non-logarithmic** values in order to obtain random variates which will be representative of the empirical data. This can be accomplished as follows: **converted value** = e^x where **x** is the lognormal value generated from the lognormal distribution.

Typical Specification Parameters: μ value, σ value, and Random Number Stream

ERLANG

$$f(x) = \frac{(\mu k)^k}{(k-1)!} x^{k-1} e^{-k\mu x}$$

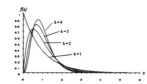

The Erlang distribution is a special case of the gamma distribution. It is frequently used in queueing systems to represent service-time distributions for various tasks. The **k** parameter value is equivalent to the α parameter in a gamma distribution. However, the values of **k** are restricted to positive integer values greater than zero. The distribution becomes an exponential distribution when **k=1**.

Suppose an operation consists of performing a single task ten times, and the time to complete each task is described by an exponential distribution with a mean parameter of **2**. Given these circumstances, the time to complete the entire operation can be represented with an Erlang distribution with a mean parameter equal to **20** (calculated as **2 x 10**) and a **k** parameter equal to **10**.

Typical Specification Parameters: $1/\mu$ mean value, **k** value, and Random Number Stream

BETA

$$f(x) = \frac{x^{\alpha_1 - 1}(1-x)^{\alpha_2 - 1}}{B(\alpha_1, \alpha_2)}$$

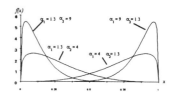

Two parameters are needed to define this distribution, α_1 and α_2. Varying their values will produce a variety of different distribution shapes. Values generated from a Beta distribution will have a range of zero to one. For this reason, it is particularly useful to represent phenomena pertaining to proportions. The proportion of defective items found in a given lot size could be described by this distribution.

The beta distribution is also used to represent the time to complete an activity when very little or no information is available about the duration of the activity. PERT (Program Evaluation and Review Technique) networks employ this distribution to determine duration times for activities within it. When used for this type of application, the values generated from this distribution must be transformed to reflect values based on estimated time parameters for completing an activity. An activity duration time is approximated in terms of a most optimistic time **o**, and a most pessimistic time **p**. A random value **x** from a beta distribution can be transformed to a random activity duration time with the following equation: **Activity duration time = o + (p - o) x.**

Typical Specification Parameters: α_1 and α_2. values, and Random Number Stream

Discrete distributions are also used in simulation models. They are employed when **x**-values for the random variable **X** are integers. Three popular discrete probability distributions are the **Poisson**, **Binomial**, and **Discrete Uniform**. Some of their common uses are described below.

POISSON $$p(x) = \frac{e^{-\lambda}\lambda^x}{x!}$$

The poisson distribution is usually associated with arrival rates. It reflects the probability associated with a finite number of successes (arrivals) occurring in a given time interval or specified area. For each integer value of a random variable **X**, there is a unique probability of occurrence associated with it.

In queueing models, the arrival rate of customers into a system is referred to as a **poisson input process**. This implies that the interarrival times of customers are exponentially distributed. The number of phone calls arriving at a switchboard each hour might be represented by a poisson distribution. The λ parameter reflects the average arrival rate per hour. Values generated from this distribution will be integer values greater than or equal to zero.

Typical Specification Parameters: mean value λ and Random Number Stream

BINOMIAL $$p(x) = \binom{n}{x} p^x q^{n-x}$$

Consider an experiment which can produce two possible outcomes, success or failure. **P** denotes the probability of success and **q** denotes the probability of failure **q=1-p**. If the probability of success remains constant with each independent repetition of the experiment, then the number of successes in **n** independent trials can be described with a binomial distribution. The number of defective items in a batch of size **n** is sometimes represented by this distribution. The random values produced by it will reflect the number of defects per batch.

Typical Specification Parameters: **p** value and Random Number Stream

DISCRETE UNIFORM $$p(x) = \frac{1}{(b-a)+1}$$

Suppose an automated storage retrieval system consists of six individual carrousels, where parts are uniformly distributed amongst them. A discrete uniform distribution with values from **1** to **6** might be used to determine the carrousel in which any given part is stored. Each value for the random variable **X** (carrousel in which a part is stored) will have an integer value within that range.

Typical Specification Parameters: Minimum value **a**, Maximum value **b**, and Random Number Stream.

Why Are Standard Distributions Used To Represent Empirical Data?

<u>**Standard distributions are used to represent empirical data distributions because they help level out data irregularities that may exist due to values missed during times of data collection.**</u> Values not observed during data collection periods can be accounted for by using standard distributions representative of the observed data.

Empirical data is frequently gathered over short time intervals. Extreme values (tail values in a distribution) may not occur during these intervals. Suppose interarrival times of customers at a bank are known to range between **0** and **60** minutes. Customer arrivals are recorded over a two day period where no interarrival times above twenty minutes are observed. Random values generated solely from the observed data will not produce values above twenty minutes. Excluding these values from an analysis can significantly influence performance responses.

Some simulation packages have the capacity to rapidly create user-defined distributions from empirical data. This feature can be very beneficial when difficulty is experienced finding representative standard distributions. User-defined distributions may require additional computational steps for each value generated. More processing time might be required when compared to the time needed with standard distributions. The net effect can be a slower running model.

What Is A "Chi-Square Goodness-Of-Fit" Test?

A <u>**Chi-Square Goodness-Of-Fit test**</u> is a statistical test that determines the level of legitimacy made with an assumption, or hypothesis. A hypothesis is a proposition which is assumed to be true without solid proof. A theoretical (standard) distribution is assumed to be a good representation of an empirical data distribution. A Chi-Square Goodness-Of-Fit test is used to check the validity of the hypothesis.

The result of the test is based on a χ^2 value calculated from the empirical data, and a critical χ^2 value obtained from a Chi-Square table. If the calculated value is less than the critical value obtained from the table, then the theoretical distribution cannot be rejected as being unrepresentative of the empirical distribution.

The χ^2 value derived from collected data is based on two factors: 1) the observed frequencies in each class interval, and 2) the expected frequencies corresponding to the same intervals in a theoretical distribution. The equation is displayed below.

$$\chi^2 = \sum_{i=1}^{k} \frac{(O_i - E_i)^2}{E_i}$$

O_i = Observed Frequency in the ith Class Interval
E_i = Expected Frequency in the ith Class Interval
k = Total Number of Class Intervals

How Is A "Chi-Square Goodness-Of-Fit" Test Performed?

The first step is to select a level of significance (also referred to as a level of confidence). It associates the risk involved with rejecting a hypothesis (a theoretical distribution is a good representation of an empirical distribution) when it is actually true. In terms of statistical jargon, this is referred to as a Type I error. A **0.05** level of significance indicates a five percent chance of making a Type I error. The "level of significance" is one of two items needed to determine critical χ^2 values. The other is the "number of degrees of freedom."

"The number of degrees of freedom in a Chi-Square Goodness-Of-Fit test is equal to the number of cells minus the number of quantities obtained from the observed data that are used in the calculations of the expected frequencies" [Walpole and Meyers (1972)]. What factors provided by the observed data are needed to calculate the expected frequencies? Expected frequency is based on a percentage of the total number of observations. Determination of the percentage factor may require such things as the mean and standard deviation from the empirical data. If this is true, then the number of degrees of freedom is equal to the total number of class intervals minus three (three factors: total observations, mean, and standard deviation). If the expected frequency is based solely on the total number of observations, then the degrees of freedom is equal to one.

The expected frequencies for each class interval can be determined from the cumulative distribution function of the theoretical distribution. Suppose a cumulative distribution function is as follows: **F(x)=x/10** for **0≤x≤10.** The number of observations expected in a class interval whose boundaries are **2** and **5** is calculated as follows: The probability of the random variable **X** being less than or equal to five **P(X≤5)** is **F(5)=5/10** or **0.5**. It is **0.2** for the **P(X≤2).** The percentage of total observations expected in the desired interval is **P(X≤5)** - **P(X≤2)** or **0.3**. If one hundred observations are collected, then it is expected that thirty **(100 x 0.3)** will fall within this interval.

Table T8B demonstrates a Goodness-Of-Fit test performed on the data shown in Table T6A on page 6-3. The hypothesized distribution (a standard probability distribution) is an exponential with a β parameter of **12.41**. The number of degrees of freedom is nine (**11** class intervals minus two factors: total observations and a mean value). The calculated χ^2 value is **2.422**. The critical value from a Chi-Square table is **16.919** (see Appendix C degrees of freedom = **9** and level of significance = **0.05**). Since the computed value is less than the critical value **(2.422 < 16.919),** there is insufficient evidence to declare the hypothesized distribution as not being a good statistical representation of the empirical distribution **(the principle is similar to being innocent until proven guilty)**. Graph G8A displays the results of this test in a histogram format.

Table T8B Chi-Square Goodness-Of-Fit Test
* (Percentage Factor multiplied by 100 Total Observations)
See Chart C8A On Page 8-11 For Calculation of P(10 ≤ **X ≤ 15)

Class Intervals	Observed Frequency O_i	Percentage Factor $P(X \le x) = 1 - e^{-x/\beta}$	* Expected Frequency E_i	$\dfrac{(O_i - E_i)^2}{E_i}$
0 - 5	36	P(X≤5) - P(X≤0) = 0.332	33.2	0.236
5 - 10	21	P(X≤10) - P(X≤5) = 0.222	22.2	0.065
10 - 15	15	** P(X≤15) - P(X≤10) = 0.148	14.8	0.003
15 - 20	7	P(X≤20) - P(X≤15) = 0.099	9.9	0.849
20 - 25	8	P(X≤25) - P(X≤20) = 0.066	6.6	0.297
25 - 30	4	P(X≤30) - P(X≤25) = 0.044	4.4	0.036
30 - 35	3	P(X≤35) - P(X≤30) = 0.030	3.0	0.000
35 - 40	3	P(X≤40) - P(X≤35) = 0.020	2.0	0.500
40 - 45	1	P(X≤45) - P(X≤40) = 0.013	1.3	0.069
45 - 50	1	P(X≤50) - P(X≤45) = 0.009	0.9	0.011
> 50	1	P(X≤) - P(X≤50) = 0.018	1.8	0.356

Calculated Chi-Square value is the summation of all $\dfrac{(O_i - E_i)^2}{E_i}$ = **2.422**

Graph G8A Observed Versus Expected Frequencies From Table T8B

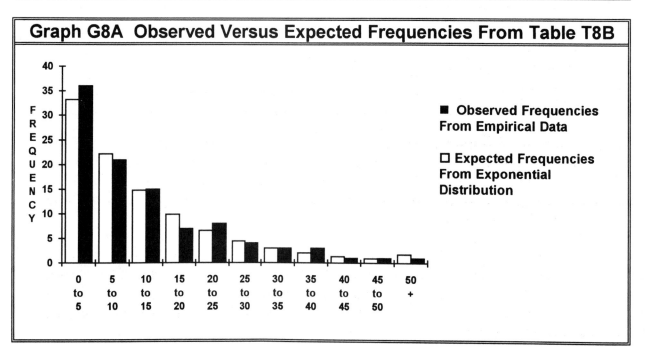

■ Observed Frequencies From Empirical Data

□ Expected Frequencies From Exponential Distribution

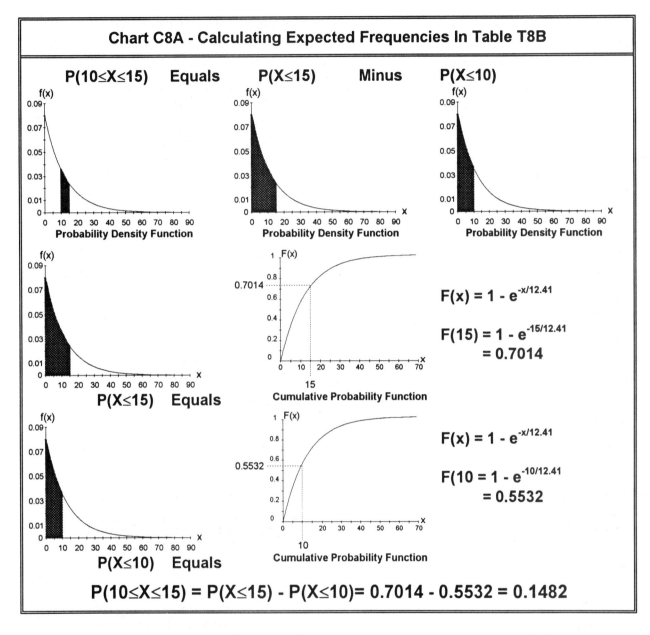

Chart C8A - Calculating Expected Frequencies In Table T8B

P(10≤X≤15) Equals P(X≤15) Minus P(X≤10)

$$F(x) = 1 - e^{-x/12.41}$$

$$F(15) = 1 - e^{-15/12.41}$$
$$= 0.7014$$

P(X≤15) Equals

$$F(x) = 1 - e^{-x/12.41}$$

$$F(10 = 1 - e^{-10/12.41}$$
$$= 0.5532$$

P(X≤10) Equals

P(10≤X≤15) = P(X≤15) - P(X≤10)= 0.7014 - 0.5532 = 0.1482

It is important to use probability distributions that are representative of the stochastic processes they are imitating. However, one should not become obsessed with finding an exact fit. Statistical inference is not a precision science. Sensitivity analyses can help reveal the input distributions which will have the greatest impact on a system's performance. More attention can be focused on those distributions.

Many simulation software packages contain features that will automatically find standard probability distributions which are representative of empirical data. There are also other software packages, such as **BestFit** by Palisade Corporation and **UniFit II** by Averill M. Law & Associates, that will perform that function. The use of these tools can substantially reduce the time required to find representative distributions.

Simulation Of A Blank Page

Chapter 9

STATISTICAL ANALYSES OF SIMULATION OUTPUT

STEPS TO LEARNING SIMULATION
1. What Is Simulation?
2. Why Simulate?
3. How Does Simulation Work?
4. Simulation Terminology
5. Simulation Products
6. Understanding Probability Distributions
7. Extracting Values From Probability Distributions
8. Finding A Distribution To Represent Data
9. Statistical Analyses Of Simulation Output
10. Building A Cost Perspective Into Simulation
11. Conducting A Successful Simulation Project
12. Avoiding Simulation Pitfalls
13. Where Can Simulation Be Used?
14. Assessing Savings From A Simulation Investment

Statistical Analyses Of Simulation Output

- Why Do Stochastic Simulations Require Multiple Model Runs And Statistical Analyses?

- What Is Statistical Inference?

- What Are "Point Estimates" And "Confidence Intervals?"

- What Is The Central Limit Theorem?

- How Are Point Estimates And Confidence Intervals Calculated?

Why Do Stochastic Simulations Require Multiple Model Runs And Statistical Analyses Of Their Output?

Multiple and independent model replications are always required with stochastic simulations. The statistical analysis of the output generated by them is a critical prerequisite for making valid conclusions. A quick review of some of the main concepts discussed in previous chapters helps clarify this important necessity.

Stochastic processes (processes composed of randomly occurring events) exist in the majority of all systems. Dynamic/stochastic simulations evaluate the impact of these processes as they interact through time. Probability distributions in conjunction with random number generators are used to create values representative of a system's stochastic behavior. The random numbers created are produced from an initial number (random number seed). Each number seed produces a unique stream of decimal random numbers (random numbers with values between 0 and 1). Decimal random numbers are translated to random values associated with a probability distribution. When number seeds are changed, a different sequence of random values are created.

Individual number seeds are assigned to each stochastic process. The results yielded from a single model replication are directly related to the number seeds selected. Changing the seed values will change the sequence of events occurring within a simulation. **Data generated from stochastic simulations is itself stochastic**. Decisions based solely on output generated from a single model replication are ill-advised. Output from multiple model replications must be analyzed with principles of statistical inference in order to make valid conclusions.

What Is Statistical Inference?

An **inference** is defined as the process of arriving at some conclusion which, though it is not logically derivable from the assumed premises, possesses some degree of probability relative to the premises. *"The theory of statistical inference may be defined to be those methods by which one makes inferences or generalizations about a population"* [Walpole and Meyers (1978)]. Principles of statistical inference are used to analyze output data created by stochastic simulation models.

There are two major areas of statistical inference. One is **estimation** and the other is **hypotheses testing**. Estimation involves establishing a degree of accuracy associated with a point estimate. What is the difference between μ (the theoretical true mean of a distribution) and $\overline{X}$ (a point estimate of a distribution's true mean)?

Hypotheses testing involves trying to make a correct decision regarding a prestated supposition. Statistical analyses provide information for accepting, or rejecting a hypothesis. The Chi-Square test described in the previous chapter, *"Finding A Distribution To Represent Data,"* is an example (See Table T8B page 8-10). An exponential distribution is theorized as being a good representation of an empirical distribution. There was not enough statistical evidence to reject the hypothesis.

What Are "Point Estimates" And "Confidence Intervals?"

A __point estimate__ is a single value used to approximate a parameter from a probability distribution. The most well known point estimate is for a mean parameter. It is the arithmetic average computed from a group of sample observations. It is usually denoted as $\overline{X}$, or $\overline{X}(n)$. The latter signifies that a point estimate is computed from __n__ sample observations. The computation of a sample's variance is another example of a point estimate. It is usually denoted as S^2, where $S^2(n)$ denotes a variance computed from __n__ sample observations.

A __confidence interval__ approximates a distribution's mean parameter in terms of a space between two values. A distribution's true mean value is described as follows: __a__ < μ < __b__, or the true mean value μ lies somewhere between the values of __a__ and __b__. If we assume the distribution from which our sample observations are taken is normally distributed (i.e., $\overline{X}(n)$ is distributed as a normal random variable), then we can calculate the respective values for __a__ and __b__ associated with a probability (confidence) of μ falling between them. As the probability becomes larger, the length of the interval becomes larger. It is better to be __95%__ confident that __10__ < μ < __15__, than __99%__ confident that __6__ < μ < __19__.

What Is The Central Limit Theorem?

The __Central Limit Theorem__ plays a major role in statistical inference. It is defined as follows: *"The distribution function of the arithmetic average of a large number of independent, identically distributed random variables is approximately equal to the standard normal distribution function (appropriately adjusted)...."* [Larson (1969)]. Let's define $\overline{X}(n)$ as an estimate of a distribution's true mean. It is computed by averaging __n__ random samples from a distribution. Assume a distribution's true mean is μ and its variance is σ^2. Suppose we make a thousand point estimates for μ, and for each estimate we calculate a value for C_n which is defined as follows:

$$C_n = \frac{\overline{X}(n) - \mu}{\sqrt{\sigma^2/n}}$$

The Central Limit Theorem tells us that the values derived for C_n will be distributed as a standard normal distribution ($\mu = 0$ and $\sigma = 1$) when the sample size __n__ is large.

This theorem is applied when analyzing simulation output. **A performance response produced from a single model replication of a stochastic simulation can be considered a single sample from the distribution of all possible responses**. Each independent model replication (replication performed with a unique set of random number streams) made thereafter produces another sample from the response distribution.

We do not know the probability distribution which represents all the possible outcomes. However, we can make estimates of the distributions true mean μ by taking random samples (responses produced from independent model replications) from the distribution.

The Central Limit Theorem tells us that when our sample size **n** is large, $\overline{X}(n)$ will be a normally distributed random variable with a mean of μ (the theoretical true mean of the distribution of all possible outcomes).

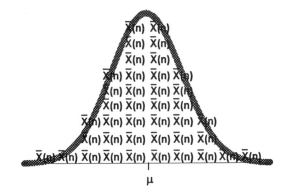

The variance of the distribution of $\overline{X}(n)$ is equal to the variance of the distribution from which the samples are taken, divided by the sample size **n**. With this information, we can use a standard normal probability density function to define confidence intervals for point estimates of μ.

How Are "Point Estimates" And "Confidence Intervals" Calculated?

A modified version of the example described in Exercise 3A of the chapter, *"How Does Simulation Work?"* is used to demonstrate the steps needed for creating confidence intervals. Exercise 3A depicts a simple queueing process. Parts arrive randomly at a queueing buffer where they are then individually processed at a machine. A discrete uniform distribution is used to describe the interarrival times at the queueing buffer. It is also used for the cycle times for each part at the machine.

In this example, the interarrival time distribution is an exponential distribution with a mean parameter of **10** minutes (β =10). The cycle times of parts at the machine have a uniform distribution (continuous) with values ranging from **5** to **11** minutes. Suppose parts only arrive during the first eight-hour shift. Parts not machined on that shift are always completed on the second, such that the queueing buffer is always empty at the start of each morning. Suppose a single part occupies four square feet of floor space while it awaits processing at the machine. How much floor space should be allocated to accommodate the WIP in the queueing buffer?

A terminating simulation is used to help answer this question. Ten independent model replications are performed. Each replication is stopped when the simulated clock time reaches **480** minutes. Random number streams for both distributions are changed on each run. The maximum and average number of parts observed in the queueing buffer are recorded per replication. The results are shown in Table T9A.

Table T9A Data Output From Terminating Model				
ith Replication	Random Number Stream for Part Arrival Distribution on the ith Replication	Random Number Stream for Machine Cycle Time Distribution on the ith Replication	Average Number of Parts Observed In the Queueing Buffer	Maximum number of Parts Observed In the Queueing Buffer
1	11	12	6.72	11
2	13	14	1.28	5
3	15	16	0.38	3
4	17	18	1.28	7
5	19	20	0.46	4
6	21	22	0.19	2
7	23	24	0.14	1
8	25	26	1.30	4
9	27	28	0.12	2
10	29	30	2.85	7

Notice the response for average part queue length produced by the respective model replications. Each is different. The importance of making multiple model replications is clearly evident. Conclusions based solely on the results of the first replication (an average of 6.72 parts in the queue) would probably not be reflective of the true mean for average part queue length. However, we can use the results from the ten model replications to make a point estimate of the true mean parameter μ. It should reveal a better estimation of the "true" average part queue length.

Table T9B on page 9-7 illustrates two statistical equations used for calculating 1) $\overline{X}(n)$ - a point estimate for a distribution's true mean parameter, and 2) $S^2(n)$ - an unbiased estimate of a distribution's variance. Both of these equations are used to find point estimates of μ and σ^2 for the output response data in Table T9A. The results are shown in Table T9C.

Table T9B   Unbiased Point Estimates of the Mean and Variance

Point Estimate of Mean μ	Unbiased Point Estimate of Variance σ^2
$$\overline{X}(n) = \frac{\sum_{i=1}^{n} X_i}{n}$$	$$S^2(n) = \frac{\sum_{i=1}^{n} [X_i - \overline{X}(n)]^2}{n-1}$$

X_i Represents The Output Response Value On The ith Model Replication

n Represents The Total Number Of Independent Model Replications Made

Table T9C   Point Estimates of μ and σ^2

ith Replication	Average Number of Parts Observed In The Queueing Buffer X_i	$[X_i - \overline{X}(10)]^2$
1	6.72	27.5415
2	1.28	0.0369
3	0.38	1.1924
4	1.28	0.0369
5	0.46	1.0241
6	0.19	1.6435
7	0.14	1.7742
8	1.30	0.0296
9	0.12	1.8279
10	2.85	1.8989
	Total = 14.72	Total = 37.00

$\overline{X}(10) = 14.72/10 = 1.472$ $S^2(10) = 37.00/9 = 4.11$

The equation for computing a confidence interval for a point estimate of μ (the theoretical true mean of a distribution) is composed of three pieces of information. They are, 1) $\overline{X}(n)$, 2) $S^2(n)$, and 3) $t_{n-1,1-\alpha/2}$. The latter is a critical value from a **student's t-distribution** with **n-1** degrees of freedom and a **1-α/2** level of confidence. The value of α determines the confidence level. A value of $\alpha=0.10$ signifies a **10** percent chance that a calculated interval will not contain the true mean parameter μ. This distribution is used when the number of independent model replications is less than **30**.

If $S^2(n)$ is a good point estimate of σ^2, then the distribution of $(\overline{x}(n)-\mu)/\sqrt{s^2(n)/n}$ is approximately distributed as a standard normal random variable. When the sample size **n** is small, **(n<30)**, the calculated value of $S^2(n)$ may not be a good estimate of σ^2. $(\overline{x}(n)-\mu)/\sqrt{s^2(n)/n}$ is then considered to be approximately distributed as a random variable from a student's t-distribution with **v** degrees of freedom (**v = n-1**).

Probability Density Function for Student's t- distribution $f(x) = \dfrac{\Gamma[(v+1)/2]}{\Gamma(v/2)\sqrt{\pi v}}(1+\dfrac{x^2}{v})^{-(v+1)/2}$

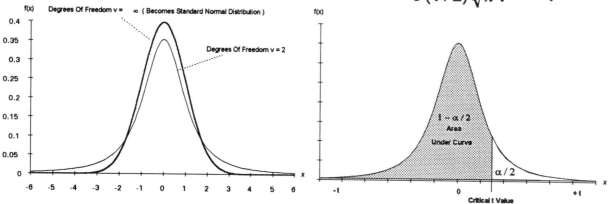

The equation for deriving a confidence interval is as follows:

$$\overline{X}(n) \pm t_{n-1,1-\alpha/2}\sqrt{\dfrac{S^2(n)}{n}}$$

Table T9D applies this equation to the average queue length data in Table T9A.

Table T9D
Calculating A Confidence Interval For The Data In Table T9C

$\overline{X}(10) = $ **1.472** $S^2(10) = $ **4.11**

$t_{n-1,\ 1-\alpha/2}$ is a value from a t-distribution table with n-1 degrees of freedom and **100(1 - α)** percent confidence (0<α<1). The t-distribution value for a **90** percent confidence interval with **9** degrees of freedom (10 replications minus one) is $t_{9,0.95} = $ 1.833 (See Appendix C for t-distribution table). A **90** percent confidence interval for the data of Table T9C is as follows:

1.472 - 1.833(0.676) < μ < 1.472 + 1.833(0.676)

0.23 < μ < 2.71

The resulting **90** percent confidence interval for a point estimate of the mean queue length is:

$$0.23 < \mu < 2.71.$$

It tells us that we can be **90** percent confident that the true mean value is contained within the interval **[0.23,2.71]**. The computed confidence interval for the maximum parts observed in the queue is **[2.7,6.4]** where $\overline{X}(n) = 4.6$ and $S^2(n) = 9.15$.

Either of the above confidence intervals can be interpreted as follows. If 100 confidence intervals are constructed in the previously described manner (ten independent model replications to produce one interval), then we can expect 90 of them to contain the true mean parameter μ. The intervals constructed in the above example are just one of the 100 confidence intervals.

If you need further clarification about the principle of a confidence interval, you can work through the following exercise.

Let's assume that the numbers in the following table are representative of all the possible output responses that might be produced from an independent model replication. The theoretical true mean μ of the distribution of all possible outcomes is **30.64** and the variance σ^2 is **52.55**.

21	21	22	22	22	22	23	23	23	23
23	23	24	24	24	24	24	25	25	25
25	25	25	25	26	26	26	26	26	26
26	27	27	27	27	27	27	27	27	28
28	28	28	28	28	28	28	28	28	29
29	29	29	29	29	29	30	30	30	30
31	31	31	31	31	31	32	33	33	33
33	33	33	34	34	34	34	34	35	35
35	36	36	36	37	38	39	39	40	40
41	41	42	42	45	46	47	52	54	58

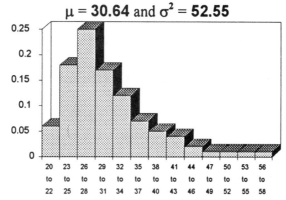

Theoretical Distribution Of All Possible Outcomes
$\mu = 30.64$ and $\sigma^2 = 52.55$

The principle of a confidence interval can be demonstrated by utilizing these numbers with the following set of instructions:

Step 1 - Make 100 small squares of paper and copy each number from the previous table onto each square of paper.

Step 2 - Put the paper squares into a container.

Step 3 - Reach into the container and randomly extract a square of paper. This is representative of making an independent model replication.

Step 4 - Record the number shown on the selected square of paper.

Step 5 - Return the selected square of paper to the container and repeat steps 3 and 4 an additional five times.

Step 6 - Calculate a 90% confidence interval for the six values recorded.

$$\overline{X}(6) \pm t_{n-1,1-\alpha/2} \sqrt{\frac{S^2(6)}{6}}$$

The critical **t** value from a t-distribution for a **90%** confidence level and **5** degrees of freedom is **2.015**.

If we perform steps three through six 100 times, then we can expect 90 of the calculated confidence intervals to contain the true mean μ (μ = **30.64** for this example). The results from ten repetitions of this exercise are displayed below:

REP	Random Sample Values	$\overline{X}(6)$	$S^2(6)$	Calculated Interval	μ Within Interval?
1	28, 37, 34, 34, 34, 21	31.33	34.26	26.52 < μ < 36.15	YES
2	42, 34, 27, 35, 23, 36	32.83	46.16	27.24 < μ < 38.42	YES
3	22, 43, 22, 28, 31, 32	29.67	61.06	23.24 < μ < 36.09	YES
4	31, 31, 25, 34, 49, 27	32.83	72.96	25.81 < μ < 39.86	YES
5	32, 31, 24, 25, 36, 26	29.00	22.40	25.11 < μ < 32.89	YES
6	27, 24, 29, 27, 22, 31	26.67	10.67	23.98 < μ < 29.35	**NO**
7	33, 24, 23, 30, 36, 28	29.00	25.60	24.84 < μ < 33.16	YES
8	50, 27, 46, 28, 27, 27	34.17	116.57	25.28 < μ < 43.05	YES
9	37, 28, 23, 37, 35, 38	33.00	37.20	27.98 < μ < 38.02	YES
10	27, 24, 41, 52, 26, 27	32.83	125.37	23.62 < μ < 42.04	YES

Chapter 10

BUILDING A COST PERSPECTIVE INTO SIMULATION

IMPROVE QUALITY & PRODUCTIVITY WITH SIMULATION

Building A Cost Perspective Into Simulation

- What Is A Cost Perspective?

- Where To Start

- The Financial People

- Synergism With Simulation

- A Cost Comparison Of Two Alternatives

- What Are The Total Costs?

- What Are Operational Costs

- How Costs Accumulate

- Simulation And The Hierarchy Of Cost Integration

- Sources Of Cost Information

- Wait Time And Carrying Costs

What Is A Cost Perspective?

Cost has many different meanings for different people. Webster's dictionary has an extensive definition of cost, but it generally boils down to *"The amount of money paid or asked for a thing,"* and *"the amount of money, time and effort to achieve an end."* Cost can also include the expenses of a course of action not taken, known as the "alternative" or opportunity costs. Opportunity costs will be an integral part in assessing the savings from an election to invest in simulation in lieu of traditional analysis methods. Chapter 14, *"Assessing Savings From A Simulation Investment,"* contains more information on this subject. This chapter focuses on incorporating a cost perspective into simulations to provide a better means for evaluating candidate solutions.

The objective of incorporating a cost perspective into simulations is to see the effects of proposed solutions in terms of cost.

With simulation, problem-solvers experiment with alternative courses of action to find the most effective solution to the problem at hand. They must work within the bounds of a myriad of technical, operational and physical constraints. In most organizations, the ultimate constraints or assumptions are the financial resources or available "budget." **There is a fiduciary duty to safeguard a company's assets and make prudent business decisions that are within the scope of an organization's financial objectives**. This applies to not only the financial people, but to all members of an organization. To a simulation user, this means that potential solutions should be evaluated based on their highest dollar benefit to a company.

The "highest dollar benefit" does not always mean the lowest cost alternative. **"Time" is a key factor in the selection of alternatives**. Are an organization's objectives geared to maximize the short term at the expense of the long term? The long term over the short term? With "time" being an essential factor, and if the goal is to maximize the short term, perhaps the highest dollar benefit can be obtained through immediate cost reduction or cost avoidance. A longer term strategy may stress the ability to increase future revenues through current expense or capital investment.

With respect to simulation, we are concerned with product or process costs related to operational planning and control. We are not concerned with the financial group's accounting and costing procedures used for preparing financial statements and external reports. **To summarize, a simulation user must present effective solutions that address not only operational, technical and physical objectives, but also the financial objectives of an organization.**

Where To Start

Given that a financial perspective is necessary, how can it be incorporated to your application? The incorporation of a cost perspective into a simulation analysis can be facilitated by answering the following four questions:

1. **What cost information is needed?**
2. **Where can the cost information be obtained?**
3. **How can cost information be processed and/or computed?**
4. **How will the cost results be interpreted from the simulation?**

Without an action plan, it is easy to get caught in a quagmire of false starts and meaningless financial data. With a plan, you have a process that can be modified to meet the project needs. Chart C10A provides information for creating such a plan.

Chart C10A WHERE TO START

Before You Begin Simulation

Steps	Source
1. Understand The Organization's OVERALL Financial Goals And Objectives	• Cost Factors Summary See- Chart C10B (page 10-5)
2. Document Specific Financial Goals And Objectives For This Simulation Project	• Project Team • Cost Factors Summary See- Chart C10B (page 10-5)
3. Determine How Costs Will Be Computed	• Hierarchy Of Cost Integration See- Chart C10G (page 10-11)

During The Simulation

Step	Source
1. Maximize The Synergism Of The Operational And Financial Aspects Of The Simulation	• Perform the FINANCIAL COROLLARY to each model building step. See - Chart C10C (page 10-6)

The first step is to understand the financial goals, objectives, assumptions, parameters and constraints associated with a project. Chart C10B (page 10-5) presents information that will attune a simulation user to a cost perspective. This information should be considered in the design and development of the proposed solutions which are being simulated. Failure to do so, may lead you to a solution that will not be in accordance with an organization's financial objectives, and will ultimately be rejected by the financial staff.

Chart C10B COST FACTORS SUMMARY

Overall Factors

TIME PERIOD
- The Ramifications Of This Project Will Extend Over What Time Period?
- Will This Project Provide A Short Term Or A Long Term Solution?
  - ⇒ *Short Term (1 year or less)*
  - ⇒ *Long Term (Over 1 year)*

CAPITAL
- Is the trend to minimize capital investment, in favor of more labor intensive solutions, or vice-versa?

This Project

- What Is The Completion Date For The Simulation Project?
- What Is The Simulation Budget For Developing, Experimenting With And Recommending A Solution?
  - ⇒ *Expense Portion (manpower, other departmental costs, etc.)*
  - ⇒ *Capital Portion (Simulation software, hardware)*
- What Is The Budget For Implementing The Resultant Solution?
  - ⇒ *Expense Portion (Engineering, design, outside services, etc.)*
  - ⇒ *Capital Portion (Machinery, equipment, physical plant, etc.)*

- **WILL THE ACCEPTABLE SIMULATION SOLUTION ALLOW:**
  - ⇒ *Increases Or Decreases In Direct Manpower Levels?*
  - ⇒ *Increases Or Decreases In Indirect Manpower Levels?*
  - ⇒ *Increases Or Decreases In Physical Space Requirements?*

The Financial People

There is often a less than productive relationship between a simulation user, and an organization's financial and or accounting group. Finance is frequently considered a "foe" rather than a "friend."

A common perception is that finance is slow to react and generally too conservative. It is probable that these perceptions arise due to limited advance communication, and limited involvement of the financial staff as part of a simulation project. The financial organization may be hesitant to react with approvals or concurrences. This is often the case, because finance is not aware of the direction and results produced by a simulation analysis. They can also appear conservative because the project direction may not be in accordance with an organization's financial objectives.

Solution: Make a friend in the financial organization. Finance should be a member of the simulation project team. Committing finance to an early involvement in a simulation project will expedite financial decision making by reducing learning curves associated with simulation analyses, and the results produced by them. These individuals will be partners and co-sponsors of simulation. As is stressed throughout this tutorial, **a simulation project is a team project. A solution derived through simulation is a group effort involving the expertise from many individuals**.

CHART C10C SIMULATION SYNERGISM	
Simulation Steps	**Financial Corollary**
1. **Formulate And Analyze The Problem**	• Establish Financial Objectives
2. **Educate Team On Basic Simulation Principles**	• Educate the team on how simulation works, how cost perspectives can be incorporated into a model, and how to interpret the results
3. **Develop Model Concept**	• Identify key assumptions and constraints • Assess and evaluate available financial data • Determine the Hierarchy of Cost Integration (See Chart C10G)
4. **Macro Data Collection**	• Collect and/or estimate preliminary cost data required for the model
5. **Model Concept And Macro Data Checkpoint**	• Does the project team concur on the cost data collected? • Are changes needed in the cost integration plan?
6. **Construct The Model**	• Incorporate cost data into model
7. **Model Verification**	• Verify cost accumulation within the model and feasibility of incorporating external financial information per the selected Hierarchy Of Cost Integration
8. **Test Model With Macro Data**	• Perform sensitivity analyses to determine the cost data which has the highest impact on the cost objectives • Collect more detailed cost data where required
9. **Model Validation**	• Compare test results with known cost and preliminary cost data • Modify and enhance as required
10. **Design Experiments For Evaluating Alternatives**	• Develop a plan for making an equitable comparison of the different candidate solutions being investigated
11. **Make Multiple Model Runs For Each Experiment**	• Determine the number of model replications needed to ascertain desired confidence levels • Make the necessary model replications and record the the results for each model run
12. **Statistical Analysis Of Output**	• Perform statistical analyses on the results generated from the model runs • Accumulate total cost and critical cost areas in accordance with financial objectives • Correlate financial results to financial and production objectives
13. **Identify Best Solutions And Document Results**	• Observe, compare and evaluate the results for each alternative investigated • Weight achievement of objectives by priority
14. **Presentation Of Results And Implementation**	• Summarize financial impacts of the various alternatives • Identify risks and opportunities

Synergism With Simulation

Synergism implies that things happen concurrently. With simulation, this involves the construction of a model that will meet both the operational and financial objectives of a project. These are not independent tasks, but rather synergistic parallel tasks. For each step in the model building process, there is a financial corollary associated with it (see Chart C10C on page 10-6)

A Cost Comparison Of Two Alternatives

This first step in developing a cost analysis of alternatives is to establish a basis for comparison. The individual and specific evaluation criteria will vary depending on a project's objectives and the nature of the project. However, a common financial denominator is the resultant total cost of the areas impacted by the proposed solutions. Assuming equivalent operational performance for each alternative (e.g., throughput, labor utilization, machine utilizations, etc.), then the alternative with the lowest total cost for the entire time period under examination would be the preferred solution.

Unfortunately, there is seldom a case when alternatives will result in equivalent operational performance. For certain scenarios, the decision-making is intuitively obvious:

> *Higher operational performance and lower total costs (Good!),*
> *and its converse*
> *Lower operational performance and higher total costs (Bad!)*

In other situations, (higher operational performance and higher total costs) the project team must weigh the differences in operational performance and the total cost differential. Cost alone should **NOT** be the sole decision making criteria.

What information is meaningful and useful?

In comparing alternatives it is necessary to determine what information is meaningful and useful. The following factors generally merit consideration in an analysis of alternatives:

- Tangible benefits (e.g., 30% increase in volume)
- Intangible benefits (e.g., increased "teamwork")
- Costs differences (cost improvements, costs avoided, additional costs)
- Resulting product cost (e.g., Unit manufacturing cost)
- Resulting total costs
- Capital costs (short term and long term)
- Trade-off of manpower vs capital costs
- Levels of existing in-house technologies and technical resources
- Training and education
- Start-up and "learning-curve" costs
- System flexibility and adaptability

Selecting Criteria On Which Costs Should Be Evaluated

The factors listed above should be considered in relation to the goals and objectives of the organization. This will help establish the criteria on which the costs should be evaluated. The key step is to prioritize the criteria (such as the factors listed above) in order of importance to the organization. This prioritized list of factors can be segmented into three groups in order of importance: items at the top of the list would have a **HIGH** priority of achievement, and the balance of the list would be **MEDIUM** or **LOW** priority.

A cost comparison of simulation alternatives will require an evaluation of the mean response values produced from multiple model replications for each alternative. When comparing the cost of alternatives, the alternative that meets more of the **HIGH** and **MEDIUM** priority requirements could indicate the preferred alternative.

What Are Total The Costs?

Total cost is a deceptively easy concept that may be quite complex. Webster's definition of cost *"...the amount of money, time and effort to achieve an end,"* can be construed in many different ways. For example, a simulation project might have an objective to increase the throughput of an existing production line to accommodate a new product. Should the total cost of the project include an allocation of the building costs for the proportionate space occupied by the production line? Some would say yes, because the building costs must be allocated in some fashion or another. Others might say no, because whether the new production line occupies more space or less space, or if it was completely eliminated, the building costs would stay the same.

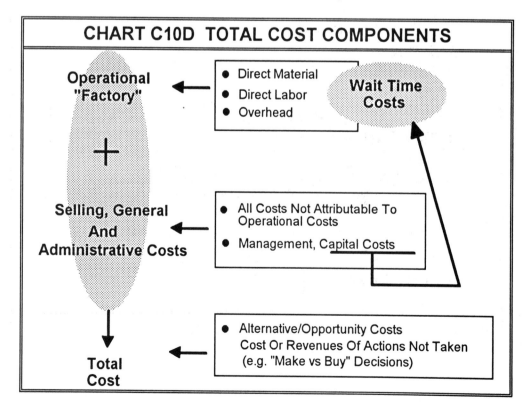

CHART C10D TOTAL COST COMPONENTS

Operational "Factory"
- Direct Material
- Direct Labor
- Overhead

Wait Time Costs

+

Selling, General And Administrative Costs
- All Costs Not Attributable To Operational Costs
- Management, Capital Costs

Total Cost
- Alternative/Opportunity Costs Cost Or Revenues Of Actions Not Taken (e.g. "Make vs Buy" Decisions)

Thus, for an analysis to be meaningful, it becomes important to ascertain which costs are included, and how those costs are to be allocated. While this may not be the responsibility of the simulation user, a general knowledge is required to recognize what is useful. Generally, simulation activities will impact Operational or Factory costs. However, they may also impact General and Administrative costs, especially if alternative solutions have significant capital outlays which will impact capital costs, depreciation, and related general and administrative costs (See Chart C10D on page 10-8)

What Are Operational Costs?

Regardless of the method for costs accumulation, the right costs must somehow be allocated or attributed to the subject product. For example, in production environments, operational cost components must be identified and charged to the product. Operational cost components traditionally consist of direct material, direct labor, and overhead (See Chart C10E).

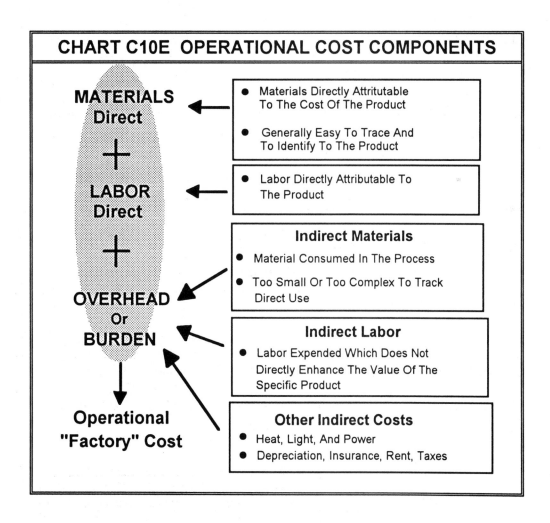

CHART C10E OPERATIONAL COST COMPONENTS

MATERIALS Direct
- Materials Directly Attritutable To The Cost Of The Product
- Generally Easy To Trace And To Identify To The Product

LABOR Direct
- Labor Directly Attributable To The Product

OVERHEAD Or BURDEN

Indirect Materials
- Material Consumed In The Process
- Too Small Or Too Complex To Track Direct Use

Indirect Labor
- Labor Expended Which Does Not Directly Enhance The Value Of The Specific Product

Other Indirect Costs
- Heat, Light, And Power
- Depreciation, Insurance, Rent, Taxes

Operational "Factory" Cost

How Costs Accumulate

Cost components must somehow be collected or "accumulated" in a consistent and meaningful manner. Traditional concepts of costing and cost allocation are changing as evidenced by the growing interest in **Activity Based Costing**. Accounting and financial changes have not kept pace with the changing technologies of manufacturing, distribution, and other areas. Pockets of financial innovation are slowly implementing academic advances in costing and cost allocation. Cost accumulation systems are briefly described in Chart C10F .

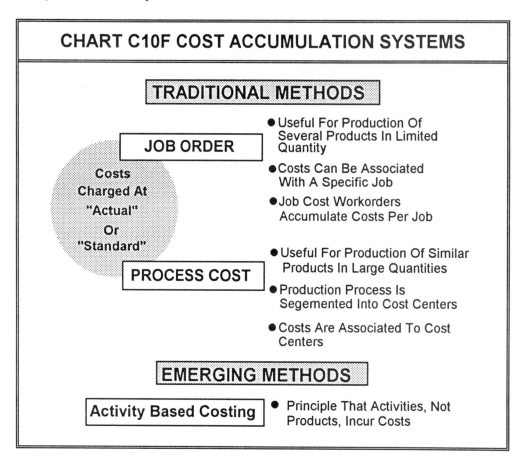

Simulation And The Hierarchy Of Cost Integration

The preceding discussions provide a brief overview of fundamental cost objectives, cost factors and cost accumulation systems. We have seen that each step in a model building process has a financial corollary. The challenge now is to find the most productive way to integrate the cost information associated with each step. There is a range or "hierarchy" for obtaining and processing cost information. At the higher end of the hierarchy, the "Optimal" solution would have concurrent processing of cost and quantitative operational data fully within a simulation model. The lower end of the hierarchy, but still a workable process, would be the processing of cost data external to the simulation model. Chart C10G summarizes these concepts.

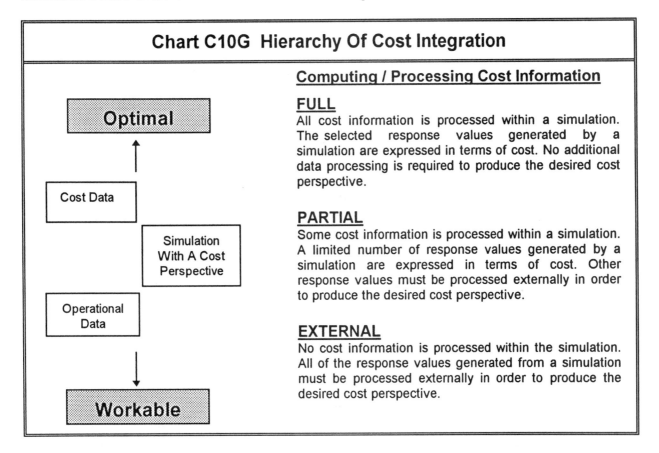

Chart C10G Hierarchy Of Cost Integration

Computing / Processing Cost Information

FULL
All cost information is processed within a simulation. The selected response values generated by a simulation are expressed in terms of cost. No additional data processing is required to produce the desired cost perspective.

PARTIAL
Some cost information is processed within a simulation. A limited number of response values generated by a simulation are expressed in terms of cost. Other response values must be processed externally in order to produce the desired cost perspective.

EXTERNAL
No cost information is processed within the simulation. All of the response values generated from a simulation must be processed externally in order to produce the desired cost perspective.

Simulation users must determine for each project, ideally with the support of the financial team members, what process will be used to integrate cost information. As with most challenges, there is no one best answer. **Select a method that will give you the desired level of cost information while minimizing the effort. Regardless of the method selected, the underlying goal is to add detail to a model only when it is deemed necessary!**

The scope, duration, and continuity of a simulation analysis must be considered when incorporating a cost perspective. "**Full**" processing may require significantly more up-front work to integrate cost data. This additional time may be justified if the model will be repeatedly utilized in the future for "what-if" analyses. However, a model which will not have repeated use may not merit the additional efforts for "**Full**" integration, and an "**External**" integration of cost data will probably be a more economical approach. Charts C10H, C10I, and C10J depict the "**Full**", "**Partial**" and "**External**" cost integration processes.

Chart C10H FULL Cost Integration

Data Requirements

- Cost information is input to the model along with traditional operation inputs

- Quantitative operational data (labor hours, rework hours, WIP levels, etc.) are generated by the simulation

Accumulation And Analysis of Cost Information

- The simulation model is designed to translate all operational information to terms of cost. All computations are performed internal to the simulation.

- Cost accumulation can be displayed with the animation provided with a simulation package

Points To Consider

- Requires extensive analysis of cost accumulation process

- Usually requires extensive use of "attribute" features

- Usually requires additional programming tasks

Chart C10I PARTIAL Cost Integration

Data Requirements

- <u>Limited</u> cost information is input to the model. Can include things such as direct material costs and direct labor rates.

- Quantitative operational data (labor hours, rework hours, WIP levels, etc.) are generated by the simulation

Accumulation And Analysis of Cost Information

- The simulation model is designed to translate limited operational information to terms of cost. Some cost computations are performed internal to the simulation, others are performed externally.

- Some cost accumulation can be displayed with the animation provided with a simulation package

Points To Consider

- Some operational data generated by a simulation must be "Exported", merged, computed and analyzed in a "Spreadsheet" or other analysis process.

- Requires overall understanding of cost accumulation process

- Provides logical division of labor with financial partner

- Cost information can be exported and processed into an organization's traditional processes for meaningful cost analysis

---

Chart C10J   EXTERNAL Cost Integration

Data Requirements

- **NO** cost information is input to the model
- Quantitative operational data (labor hours, rework hours, WIP levels, etc.) are generated by the simulation

Accumulation And Analysis of Cost Information

- The simulation model has no cost information integrated into it. All cost computations and analyses are performed external to the simulation.

Points To Consider

- All operational data generated by a simulation must be "Exported", merged, computed and analyzed in a "Spreadsheet" or other analysis process.
- Requires minimal understanding of cost accumulation process
- Cost information can be exported and processed into an organization's traditional processes for meaningful cost analysis

---

Sources Of Cost Information

Most cost information is relatively straight forward: a quantity multiplied by a value. For example:

	Quantity	×	Dollar Value
Direct Material Cost =	Parts	×	Unit Cost
Direct Labor =	Hours	×	Hourly Rate
Overhead =	Unit	×	Overhead Rate

A simulation user is concerned with obtaining quantity and dollar value information in the most expeditious manner. Some information is available directly from the simulation model (quantity throughput, labor hours earned, etc.). Other information must be input to the simulation model, or processed externally depending on the hierarchy of cost integration. Once again, teamwork with your financial partner will expedite obtaining this information. Chart C10K and Chart C10L on page 10-14 depict some sources for cost information.

Chart C10K SOURCES OF COST INFORMATION

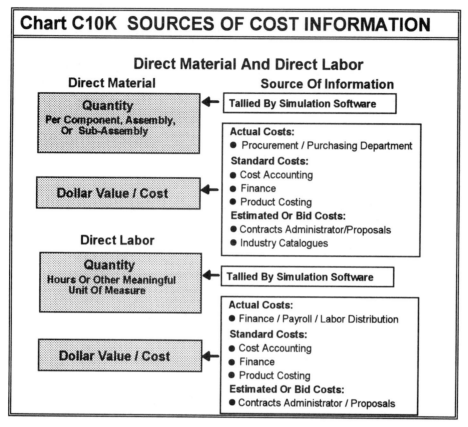

Direct Material And Direct Labor

Direct Material

Source Of Information

Quantity
Per Component, Assembly, Or Sub-Assembly ← Tallied By Simulation Software

Dollar Value / Cost ←
- **Actual Costs:**
  - Procurement / Purchasing Department
- **Standard Costs:**
  - Cost Accounting
  - Finance
  - Product Costing
- **Estimated Or Bid Costs:**
  - Contracts Administrator/Proposals
  - Industry Catalogues

Direct Labor

Quantity
Hours Or Other Meaningful Unit Of Measure ← Tallied By Simulation Software

Dollar Value / Cost ←
- **Actual Costs:**
  - Finance / Payroll / Labor Distribution
- **Standard Costs:**
  - Cost Accounting
  - Finance
  - Product Costing
- **Estimated Or Bid Costs:**
  - Contracts Administrator / Proposals

CHART C10L SOURCES OF COST INFORMATION

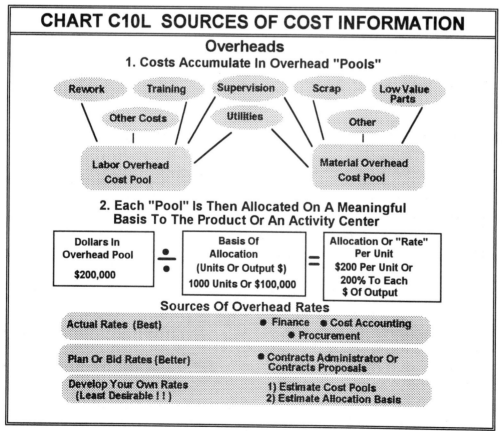

Overheads
1. Costs Accumulate In Overhead "Pools"

Rework   Training   Supervision   Scrap   Low Value Parts

Other Costs   Utilities   Other

Labor Overhead Cost Pool   Material Overhead Cost Pool

2. Each "Pool" Is Then Allocated On A Meaningful Basis To The Product Or An Activity Center

Dollars In Overhead Pool	÷	Basis Of Allocation (Units Or Output $)	=	Allocation Or "Rate" Per Unit
$200,000		1000 Units Or $100,000		$200 Per Unit Or 200% To Each $ Of Output

Sources Of Overhead Rates

Actual Rates (Best)   ● Finance   ● Cost Accounting   ● Procurement

Plan Or Bid Rates (Better)   ● Contracts Administrator Or Contracts Proposals

Develop Your Own Rates (Least Desirable ! !)   1) Estimate Cost Pools   2) Estimate Allocation Basis

Wait Time And Carrying Costs

Reducing wait time is a key objective in any world class manufacturing environment. The ramifications of wait time can be extensive. Chart C10M displays some areas impacted by wait time. Carrying costs have traditionally been hidden costs and are not necessarily included in a production decision making process. However, increasing concerns for the "total product cost" picture have triggered an increased awareness of carrying costs. Simulation is one of the best tools for measuring a key cause of carrying costs - wait time.

CHART C10M   WAIT TIME IMPACTS

AREA	IMPACTS
• Inventory Carrying Costs	• Interest, Other Costs
• Physical Space Requirements	• Expense, Capital, Manpower
• "Buffer"/Queueing Equipment	• Expense, Capital
• "Buffer"/Queueing Labor	• Manpower Expense
• Quality/Early Defect Identification	• Rework Expense, Material Cost
• Longer Makespan	• Customer Lead Times
• Production Capacity	• Revenue, Capital
• Inventory Turnover	• Revenue
• Inventory Control	
• Operational	• Expense
• Financial	• Expense

What Is Carrying Cost?

Carrying cost is the cost to own an asset. Carrying costs are directly related to the value of the assets and the length of time those assets remain in a process. The definition and calculation of carrying cost will differ from company to company. It is advisable to obtain the carrying cost directly from the financial organization. The cost will usually be expressed as an amount (e.g., $150 per part, per year) or as an annual percent of the part cost (e.g., 30% per year).

Carrying costs include the costs related to the 1) inventory item, and 2) the physical space occupied by the inventory item. Costs related to the inventory item include: the percentage return on the dollars invested in inventory, insurance, taxes and other direct factors. Costs related to the physical space occupied by the inventory item include: rental or ownership costs, depreciation, taxes, insurance, maintenance, utilities, etc. Often, many of the carrying cost factors such as insurance, taxes, rental or ownership costs may already be included in the overhead rates that are allocated to the inventory costs. These costs should be excluded from the carrying cost calculation.

The following example shows a simplified carrying cost calculation for a part in work-in-process (WIP) at a single operation:

> ## Assumptions For Calculating A Carrying Cost
> Initial Material Cost = $1000/part;
> Material Added = $1000/part;
> Labor Added = $1000/part;
> Allocated Overhead = $1000/part;
> Assume Average Production Rate of 25 Parts Per Month
> Average Wait Time Per Part (no-value added) = 1 month
> Total WIP Cost Per Month = $4000 x 25 = $100000
>
> Return on money invested in inventory = 25% per year (Assumes all other inventory and physical space costs are included in the overhead rate)
>
> Carrying cost = $2083 per month   ($100000 x 25% x 1/12 (1 month)) or 2.083% per month ($2083/$100000).

Weighted Average Work-In-Process Costs

An asset in work-in-process has a value (cost) that increases as it moves through the production process. Given a makespan or fixed production cycle time, it may be advantageous to add high dollar material and labor near the end of the makespan to reduce the weighted average cost during the makespan. This weighted average cost can impact carrying costs, especially in the case of high dollar and long makespans (e.g., aircraft, satellites, etc.). In such instances, including carrying cost factors in a simulation model may provide valuable financial information which can influence the production process.

Carrying Cost Impacts

It is advisable to estimate the sensitivity of carrying costs prior to conducting an in-depth analysis. Sometimes, a significant improvement in wait time and a resultant reduction in carrying costs will have a nominal impact on total costs. Impacts and sensitivities can be estimated by **1) approximating the carrying cost percentage, 2) computing total dollar impacts, and 3) comparing the ratio of carrying costs to total costs**. If the estimated impacts are not significant, your time may be better spent elsewhere.

Chapter 11

CONDUCTING A SUCCESSFUL SIMULATION PROJECT

Chapter 11 Has Fourteen Sub-Chapters

STEPS TO LEARNING SIMULATION
1. What Is Simulation?
2. Why Simulate?
3. How Does Simulation Work?
4. Simulation Terminology
5. Simulation Products
6. Understanding Probability Distributions
7. Extracting Values From Probability Distributions
8. Finding A Distribution To Represent Data
9. Statistical Analyses Of Simulation Output
10. Building A Cost Perspective Into Simulation
11. Conducting A Successful Simulation Project
12. Avoiding Simulation Pitfalls
13. Where Can Simulation Be Used?
14. Assessing Savings From A Simulation Investment

STEPS TO CONDUCTING A SUCCESSFUL SIMULATION PROJECT
1. Formulate And Analyze The Problem
2. Educate The Team On Basic Simulation Principles
3. Develop Model Concept
4. Macro Data Collection
5. Model Concept And Macro Data Review
6. Construct The Model
7. Model Verification
8. Test The Model With Macro Data
9. Model Validation
10. Design Experiments For Evaluating Alternatives
11. Make Multiple Model Runs For Each Alternative
12. Statistical Analysis Of Output
13. Identify Best Solutions And Document Results
14. Presentation Of Results And Implementation

Chapter 11.1

FORMULATE AND ANALYZE THE PROBLEM

STEPS TO CONDUCTING A SUCCESSFUL SIMULATION PROJECT
1. Formulate And Analyze The Problem
2. Educate The Team On Basic Simulation Principles
3. Develop Model Concept
4. Macro Data Collection
5. Model Concept And Macro Data Review
6. Construct The Model
7. Model Verification
8. Test The Model With Macro Data
9. Model Validation
10. Design Experiments For Evaluating Alternatives
11. Make Multiple Model Runs For Each Alternative
12. Statistical Analysis Of Output
13. Identify Best Solutions And Document Results
14. Presentation Of Results And Implementation

Formulate And Analyze The Problem

- What Constitutes The Problem?

- What Are The Objectives Of The Project?

- What Are The Criteria For Evaluating Performance?

- What Are The Assumptions?

- What Are The Input Parameters?

- What Are The Restrictions On Solution Variables?

- Manpower Time And Cost Estimations For The Project

What Constitutes The Problem?

The first and most fundamental step in any problem-solving process is defining the problem. It is very difficult to solve a problem when there are uncertainties regarding what the problem is. Determining where we are and where we want to be is the starting point in any problem-solving process. The problem statement should be clearly defined and known by all members of the project team.

"Express a problem in a precise and systematic form, but keep a broad mind when doing it. Include as much of the total problem as the importance of the situation and organizational boundaries will permit. The more a total problem is divided into sub-problems to be solved separately, the less effective the total solution is likely to be" [Krick (1976)].

What Are The Objectives Of The Project?

A simulation project begins with the establishment of clear objectives. Objectives are one of the primary design factors in a simulation model. **Model design cannot begin until objectives have been determined. Objectives should be clearly stated and understood by the decision-makers and all the people involved with the simulation effort.**

It is important not to formulate vague objectives. For example, an objective such as, "We are simulating to improve the efficiency of the manufacturing system," is very nebulous. Try to express objectives as questions. What issues will be answered when a simulation study is completed? Examples for a manufacturing system might be as follows: What impact will lot size have on WIP related costs? How many AGVs are required to achieve a specified production rate? Will a certain workcell strategy decrease product makespans?

What Are The Criteria For Evaluating Performance?

A criterion is a standard of judgment. It is sometimes referred to as a performance index. Criteria tell us how an alternative's effectiveness will be evaluated. Like objectives, criteria needs to be established prior to building a simulation model. A model is designed in a manner that will reflect the performance of a system in terms of selected criteria. A few examples of some typical manufacturing criteria are throughput, WIP levels, queueing time, equipment/labor utilizations, and product makespans.

The most universal criterion is probably money. Each of the previously mentioned criteria can be translated to dollar costs. It is generally easier to evaluate and present results when they are expressed in terms of dollars. This is especially true for management presentations. Managers are primarily concerned with profits. What can they expect to gain from implementing a given alternative? This is why it is often advantageous to build a cost perspective into models. The most qualified people for providing cost information are financial personnel. They should be actively involved when cost objectives are being established for a model. The importance or weight of each criterion should also be determined. Is a cost criterion more important than a product cycle time criterion? If so, then by how much? The weights of each criterion are essential for evaluating alternatives.

What Are The Assumptions?

Assumptions are a common and required element in almost every type of analysis. A manufacturing assumption might be the time between breakdowns on a piece of equipment. Historical data frequently does not exist for determining this factor. A certain distribution is then assumed to be representative of it.

Assumptions can simplify a model building process, but they can also influence the results. It is better to start with many assumptions, and to reduce them at a point when deemed necessary. An assumption is good until it is discovered that it significantly impacts simulation results. When this occurs, it becomes obligatory to reevaluate that assumption.

Like criteria, assumptions must be documented and agreed upon at the onset of a project. Additional assumptions will often be made during the course of a project. They too, need to be documented. Models of hypothetical systems will generally have more assumptions than those of existing systems.

What Are The Input Parameters?

Input parameters are the variable factors which can influence the performance of a system. Some examples for manufacturing systems are lot sizes, quantity of equipment, quantity of labor, conveyor speeds, scheduling strategies, and machine cycle times. Changing the values of the input variables can cause changes in a model's performance.

Input parameters are often subjected to constraints. Perhaps a conveyor speed must be below a certain limit in order to avoid damaging packages traveling on it. Constraints, if any, should be identified for each input variable.

What Are The Restrictions On Solution Variables?

"A **restriction** is a solution characteristic previously fixed by decision, nature, law, or any other source the problem-solver must honor" [Krick (1976)]. Alternative courses of action may be subjected to limitations of manpower, equipment, material, time, or cost. Restrictions, like constraints, should be identified at the onset of a project.

Beware of <u>**fictitious restrictions**</u>. A fictitious restriction is an invented restraint. It is assumed to exist, when in reality it does not. One of the best ways to demonstrate a fictitious restriction is to connect the nine dots in the following diagram with no more than four straight lines, and without removing your pen from the paper while drawing the lines. The solution to this problem can be found on page 11.1-8.

The solution to this problem can be found on page 11.1-8.

```
  •   •   •

  •   •   •

  •   •   •
```

Manpower, Time, And Cost Estimations For The Project?

Two questions frequently expressed at the onset of a simulation project are, "How long will it take?" and "How much will it cost?" The answer to both questions depends on many factors that are unique to each project. A model that contains very little detail can be constructed more quickly than a model that contains a lot of detail. An experienced model builder can usually build a model more quickly than a person who is just beginning. The simulation aptitude of the people involved with the simulation effort can also impact the project duration. A project's duration and costs will vary with each project.

The best method for estimating the time and costs associated with a simulation project is fairly straight forward. The steps are 1) define the tasks required for completing the project, 2) estimate the time required to complete the tasks, and 3) assign the labor resources who will be responsible for completing each task. Chart C11.1A depicts an elementary form of a simulation milestone chart. Some of the major steps in a simulation project are shown. Task durations, manpower requirements, and costs should be estimated for each step. The results should be presented to the decision-makers. If approved, the decision-makers must be willing to commit the necessary resources to complete the tasks.

Chart C11.1A Simulation Project Milestone Chart			
TASK DESCRIPTION	DURATION	RESOURCES	COSTS
Formulate And Analyze The Problem	_____	_____	_____
Educate Team On Basic Simulation Principles	_____	_____	_____
Develop Model Concept	_____	_____	_____
Macro Data Collection	_____	_____	_____
Model Concept & Macro Data Checkpoint	_____	_____	_____
Construct The Model	_____	_____	_____
Model Verification	_____	_____	_____
Test Model With Macro Data	_____	_____	_____
Model Validation	_____	_____	_____
Design Experiments For Alternatives	_____	_____	_____
Make Multiple Runs For Each Alternative	_____	_____	_____
Statistical Analysis Of Output	_____	_____	_____
Identify Best Solutions And Document Results	_____	_____	_____
Presentation Of Results	_____	_____	_____

Solution to Fictitious Restriction Problem on page 11.1-7.

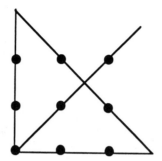

Chapter 11.2

EDUCATE TEAM ON BASIC SIMULATION PRINCIPLES

STEPS TO CONDUCTING A SUCCESSFUL SIMULATION PROJECT
1. Formulate And Analyze The Problem
2. Educate The Team On Basic Simulation Principles
3. Develop Model Concept
4. Macro Data Collection
5. Model Concept And Macro Data Review
6. Construct The Model
7. Model Verification
8. Test The Model With Macro Data
9. Model Validation
10. Design Experiments For Evaluating Alternatives
11. Make Multiple Model Runs For Each Alternative
12. Statistical Analysis Of Output
13. Identify Best Solutions And Document Results
14. Presentation Of Results And Implementation

Educate The Team On Basic Simulation Principles

- Do The People Involved With The Project Have A Basic Understanding Of Simulation Principles?

- What Do Project Participants Need To Know?

Do The People Involved With The Project Have A Basic Understanding Of Simulation Principles?

<u>An important, yet often overlooked step in a simulation project is training</u>. The simulation user (model builder) should obviously have a good comprehension of simulation methodologies and principles. What about the other people involved; managers, engineers, operational personnel and those who will be affected by the results of the analysis? It is probably fair to say that very few people typically possess a firm grasp of what simulation is, how it works, or what it can do. **Educating project participants on simulation fundamentals can embellish findings, reduce project durations and make selling and implementing solutions much easier**.

Many operational personnel are reluctant to provide reliable information unless they know where and how their input will be used. Quality data promotes valid results. It is a vital component in any study. <u>Data contributors who have an elementary knowledge of simulation methodologies usually show greater project enthusiasm than those who do not.</u>

Simulation education fosters cooperation between project participants. It can be accomplished with a brief training session at the onset of a project. Without such a session, the model builder can find himself or herself repeatedly explaining simulation to each individual being solicited for information, and to each person affected by the results.

Training should not be limited to only operational personnel. Many managers, engineers and financial personnel are not acquainted with this tool. The lack of familiarity can produce reactions such as, "Simulation is not needed with this project." or, "Let's not be lulled into believing simulation results." The latter is especially true if the findings do not concur with previously conceived solutions.

The success of any project depends on the magnitude and quality of the contributions provided by the participants. <u>Educating people on what simulation is, why it is needed, how it works, and how every employee is an integral part of its success is a critical step in the model building process</u>. A brief, informative training session can sometimes be the difference between a successful project and a non-successful project.

What Do Project Participants Need To Know?

The level of simulation knowledge needed by various participants in a simulation project varies. Table T11.2A on page 11.2-4 depicts six subjects related to simulation: **What Is Simulation?, Why Simulation Is Being Used, How Simulation Works, Model Building Steps, Simulation Statistical Analyses,** and **How To Use A Simulation Package**. The table relates the skill level required by project participants for each of the respective subjects.

Skill levels are classified as 1) <u>Good Working Knowledge</u> - comprehends key concepts and principles, can apply concepts, and can educate others; 2) <u>Fundamental Understanding</u> -

understands the key concepts and principles; and 3) **Appreciation** - can recognize the importance and worth associated with a simulation subject area. The training time needed to achieve the various skill levels in each participant category will depend upon the backgrounds of the individuals involved. <u>The estimated time requirements shown in the table assume no prior knowledge of simulation.</u>

Table T11.2A What People Need To Know About Simulation			
	Participants In A Simulation Project		
Subject	**Model Builder**	**Management and Financial Personnel**	**Operational Personnel**
What Is Simulation?	Good Working Knowledge	Good Working Knowledge	Appreciation
Why Simulation Is Being Used	Good Working Knowledge	Good Working Knowledge	Appreciation
How Simulation Works	Good Working Knowledge	Fundamental Understanding	Appreciation
Model Building Steps	Good Working Knowledge	Good Working Knowledge	Appreciation
Simulation Statistical Analyses	Good Working Knowledge	Appreciation	Appreciation
How To Use A Simulation Package	Good Working Knowledge	Fundamental Understanding	Appreciation
Training Time Required	**24-40 Hours**	**3-8 Hours**	**1-2 Hours**

Chapter 11.3

DEVELOP MODEL CONCEPT

STEPS TO CONDUCTING A SUCCESSFUL SIMULATION PROJECT
1. Formulate And Analyze The Problem
2. Educate The Team On Basic Simulation Principles
3. Develop Model Concept
4. Macro Data Collection
5. Model Concept And Macro Data Review
6. Construct The Model
7. Model Verification
8. Test The Model With Macro Data
9. Model Validation
10. Design Experiments For Evaluating Alternatives
11. Make Multiple Model Runs For Each Alternative
12. Statistical Analysis Of Output
13. Identify Best Solutions And Document Results
14. Presentation Of Results And Implementation

Develop Model Concept

- What Is The Modeling Strategy?

- How Much Detail Is Required?

- How Will The Model Communicate?

- How Much Time Should Be Spent Customizing Background Layouts And Icons?

- What Elements In A System Should Be Modeled With "Black Boxes?"

- How Will Data Be Input To A Model?

What Is The Modeling Strategy?

Modeling strategy involves making decisions regarding how a system should be represented in terms of the capabilities and elements provided with a simulation package. Discrete event modeling may be advantageous over continuous event modeling. Maybe a combination of both is required. Will terminating or steady-state models be used? Should individual entities be modeled, or groups of entities? **The overall strategy should focus on finding a model concept that minimizes the simulation effort while ensuring that all objectives of the study are met.**

When an existing system is going to be simulated, a structured walk-through of the areas involved in the study is an excellent way to initiate a modeling strategy. The walk-through should be conducted with the model builder, key members of the project team (decision-makers), and system experts from the respective areas.

How Much Detail Is Required?

The level of detail put into a model is dependent upon the availability of existing data and other information pertinent to a study. A model of a hypothetical system would have less detail than a model of an existing system. **The primary focus should be on capturing the conditions and facts that can have a bearing on the objectives of a simulation.**

There is a point of diminishing returns regarding the amount of detail that should be put into a model. **Results will not necessarily become more accurate as detail is increased. In many cases, it will become less.** Trying to create a model which has a one-to-one relationship with a target system (system being modeled) is a futile effort which often leads to simulation failures. It is a common mistake made by many first-time model builders. **The best rule is simply, "Increase the level of detail only when it is necessary."**

How Will The Model Communicate?

Communicating model logic and results is a vital element in every simulation analysis. A model's credibility is influenced by its ability to express itself. On-screen graphical animation features provided with many simulation packages are an excellent means of communicating. Conveying system flows, explaining alternatives, and identifying potential drawbacks with an alternative are significantly embellished with this feature. It should be emphasized that the latter is only good for identifying problem areas. **Response data must be statistically analyzed in order to understand their magnitudes, and to make recommendations for improvements.**

In absence of on-screen animation, the simulation user must rely primarily on communication aids such as charts, graphs and tables. Response data produced by simulation models can frequently be exported to other graphical/analytical software packages such as Excel™, Lotus 1-2-3™, and dBase™. When these alternatives are being utilized, consideration must be directed towards designing file formats for simulation output which will be compatible with input requirements of other software packages.

How Much Time Should Be Spent Customizing Background Layouts And Icons?

Many simulation packages give model builders the ability to customize graphical icons and screen backgrounds. The time spent utilizing these features is a worthy effort as long as it is not overdone. Graphical icons and background layouts can significantly enhance a model's ability to communicate. They can make animation more realistic. Conversely, too much animation can be detrimental to a model. Unnecessary animation is a wasted effort and can detract from the overall purpose of a model. **The level of animation should be just enough to effectively communicate a simulation's key objectives**.

What Elements In A System Should Be Modeled With "Black Boxes?"

"Black boxes" are used to represent elements in a system where information regarding the operation of an element is either 1) Not feasible to obtain, or 2) Does not require detailed modeling. Parts fabricated at an off-site vendor's facility is a good example. It would not be practical to model a vendor's manufacturing facility. A black box approach is a better way to represent it. The only properties of a black box are that something goes in and something comes out. What happens inside is not considered. The only concern is the amount of time spent in the box.

How Will Data Be Input To A Model?

One of simulation's main advantages is its ability to perform "what if" type analyses. Input parameters are varied to determine their impact on the system criteria. How easy is it to change the input parameters of the model? Will the end-users of the model be able to change the input parameters to test future alternatives? These considerations must be addressed when developing the model concept.

It is usually advantageous to create data input files which can be easily modified in a spreadsheet type manner. The data files can then be read into a model. A unique data file is created for each alternative investigated. Sometimes it is possible to have the model prompt the user for values of input parameters. This approach is good when the number of input parameters is small.

MACRO DATA COLLECTION

STEPS TO CONDUCTING A SUCCESSFUL SIMULATION PROJECT

1. Formulate And Analyze The Problem
2. Educate The Team On Basic Simulation Principles
3. Develop Model Concept
4. **Macro Data Collection**
5. Model Concept And Macro Data Review
6. Construct The Model
7. Model Verification
8. Test The Model With Macro Data
9. Model Validation
10. Design Experiments For Evaluating Alternatives
11. Make Multiple Model Runs For Each Alternative
12. Statistical Analysis Of Output
13. Identify Best Solutions And Document Results
14. Presentation Of Results And Implementation

Macro Data Collection

- What Is Macro Data?

- What Are The Interrelationships And Rules That Govern The Dynamics Of The System?

- Where Are The Potential Data Sources?

- Is The Data Gathering Effort Greater With Simulation Than With Other Problem-solving Tools?

- Collecting Macro Data For Cost Perspectives?

What Is Macro Data?

"Macro data" is fundamental facts, information, and statistics derived through historical records, experience, or by calculation. It is acquired by taking a high level perspective of a system being modeled. Macro data is not concerned with particulars. Its purpose is to 1) provide a basis for establishing a model's input parameters and 2) to pinpoint input parameters that will require detailed (micro) data collection.

Suppose you are trying to establish a cycle time distribution for a certain operation, and no historical data is available. You might quickly estimate the cycle time with a triangular distribution based on a minimum, maximum, and most likely time. Sensitivity analyses (see chapter 11.8 *"Test Model With Macro Data"*) carried out after a model is operational can determine if an input parameter significantly influences a model's output with respect to performance criteria. If it does, then more detailed data collection may be warranted.

What Are The Inter-relationships And Rules That Govern The Dynamics Of A System?

Process flow charts are good tools for determining system interrelationships and the rules that govern their dynamics. They sequentially reflect each step and procedure involved in a process. Questions regarding **who, what, when, where, why,** and **how** are correlated for each step. Elements whose performances are influenced or controlled by other elements are identified. Creating these charts, forces a thorough examination of a process. The information acquired becomes the foundation and structure for building a model.

Chart C11.4A on page 11.4-4 is an example of a basic process flow chart. A derivative of this type of chart is illustrated in Chart C11.4B. A process is now defined in terms of steps. Each step is divided into the basic acts generally performed with any operation. They are **store, do operation, store,** and **move to next operation**. More detailed information such as lot sizes, tooling and labor requirements, or other pertinent data can be included with each step.

Many manufacturing systems contain multiple part types, each having a unique process routing sequence. Some simulation packages contain features for creating routing files for individual parts or families of parts. Process flow charts or other data sheets should be designed in a format that is advantageous to creating these files. **Try to collect data in a configuration that is compatible to the input features of the simulation package.**

Where Are The Potential Data Sources?

System experts are one of the best information sources. They are the people who have hands-on experience or familiarity with a system, or system component. Other sources are historical reports, reference books and computer databases.

Data sources need to be documented. It helps establish model credibility. The question, "Where did you get your data?" usually surfaces at some point in all analytical studies. A response of, "I'm not sure." or, "Can I get back to you later?" does not promote confidence.

Data can be collected in many ways. It is usually beneficial to create standard forms for gathering similar types of data. This is particularly true when several people are collecting common information from numerous sources.

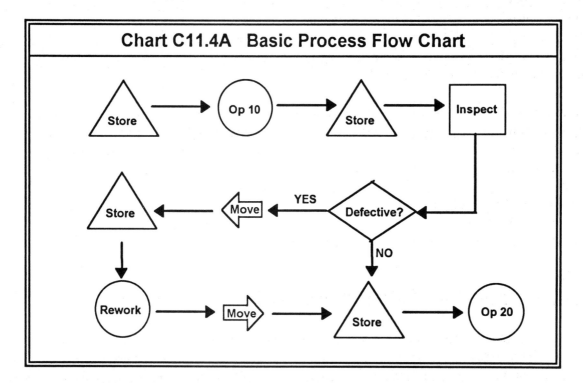

Chart C11.4A   Basic Process Flow Chart

Chart C11.4B   Step Flow Chart

| Step # | STORE | PERFORM OPERATION | | | | STORE | MOVE |
	Store	Operation Description	Machine Name	Setup Time	Cycle Time	Store	Move
1	Rack1A	Mill Top	Mill1	* U(0.3,0.6)	T(0.5,0.6,0.9)	Rack1B	Mat'lHand1
2	Rack3A	Bore Holes	MachB	0.20	0.50		
3	Conveyor2	Press Bearings	Press1	U(0.1,0.3)	0.25	Rack6B	Mat'lHand2
4	Rack9A	Drill Holes	Dr1 or Dr2	None	0.10	Rack9B	Mat"lHand1

* U(0.3,0.6) denotes a Uniform Distribution with values between 0.3 and 0.6 hours

T(0.5,0.6,0.9) denotes a Triangular Distribution with values between 0.3 and 0.9 hours and a mode of 0.6

Is The Data Collection Effort Greater With Simulation Than With Other Problem-solving Tools?

People who have not been directly involved with a simulation study will probably assume that data gathering is significantly greater with simulation than with other problem solving approaches. In reality, **the information collected for a simulation study is the same information collected for almost any heuristic problem-solving method.** Given this fact, the time required to collect data remains approximately the same for each problem-solving approach. This misconception is probably a by-product of the model building effort associated with yesterday's simulation packages. In the past, simulation generally involved lengthy programming efforts. Sometimes this old image is mistakenly associated with data collection.

Data collection/analysis is an important and essential step in any problem-solving process. Candidate solutions are only as good as the data from which they are derived. Few will disagree that data collection can be time consuming and sometimes expensive. However, it is an essential ingredient for finding successful solutions. Decision-makers often want answers to problems, but are unwilling to commit resources to collect adequate information pertaining to the problems. When this occurs, opinions are frequently substituted for facts. A major shortcoming of opinion based data can be expressed with a single quotation by Utvich, *"One accurate measurement is worth a thousand expert opinions."*

Collecting Macro Data For Cost Perspectives

Building financial information into a model can substantially contribute to a model's effectiveness. It helps pinpoint areas where the greatest cost savings can be realized. Financial personnel are the best sources for providing cost related information. Their involvement can significantly improve a model's credibility and presentation value.

Wait time is an example of a business criterion that can take on new meaning when translated to dollar costs. The cost incurred for waiting (storing parts or other entities in process) can be one of the major contributors to a process or product's total cost. Many manufacturing models do not present this factor in terms of cost. Wait time is solely expressed in terms of hours, days, and months. Converting the time to dollar costs can lead to different conclusions. Chapter 10, *"Building A Cost Perspective Into A Simulation"* elaborates on this subject. Some of the basic ingredients that compose a wait time cost are discussed in that chapter.

Simulation Of A Blank Page

Chapter 11.5

MODEL CONCEPT AND MACRO DATA CHECK POINT

STEPS TO CONDUCTING A SUCCESSFUL SIMULATION PROJECT
1. Formulate And Analyze The Problem
2. Educate The Team On Basic Simulation Principles
3. Develop Model Concept
4. Macro Data Collection
5. Model Concept And Macro Data Review
6. Construct The Model
7. Model Verification
8. Test The Model With Macro Data
9. Model Validation
10. Design Experiments For Evaluating Alternatives
11. Make Multiple Model Runs For Each Alternative
12. Statistical Analysis Of Output
13. Identify Best Solutions And Document Results
14. Presentation Of Results And Implementation

Model Concept And Macro Data Review

- Does The Project Team Concur On System Flows And Other Macro Data?

- Do The Model Objectives Concept Or Assumptions Need To Be Changed?

Does The Project Team Concur On System Flows And Other Macro Data?

Prior to commencing the actual model building, it is important to review the macro data that has been collected. It will help ensure a concurrence on the findings. This is best accomplished with a group meeting attended by all involved parties (managers, decision makers, engineers, data contributors, and financial personnel). Inaccuracies can be discovered and corrected much faster through a group review of the data. **The group meeting will help establish team ownership in the model**.

The creation of system flow charts can often reveal operations in a process where procedures are absent or unclear. What determines the priority for performing an operation when numerous assemblies are competing for the same machine, tooling, or labor? Sometimes there are no written rules for making these decisions. An operator's opinion or the vocal capabilities of a manager frequently determine the outcome. Conditions such as these must be addressed when they are perceived to influence the objectives of a model. Procedural decisions must be made and the results incorporated into the model concept.

The purpose of this step is NOT for adding detail to a model. Its intent is to clear up any major disagreements which may exist in the macro data or the model concept. At this stage, the project team should NOT be concerned with identifying elements that may require detailed data collection. This information will be revealed during sensitivity analyses performed after the model is functional.

Do The Model Objectives, Concept, Or Assumptions Need To Be Changed?

Macro data reviews can cause changes to model objectives, model concepts, and model assumptions. Data collection efforts often spawn new ideas for potential improvements. Testing the effectiveness of these alternatives may become a new objective for the study. Perhaps more than one model is needed to effectively satisfy all the objectives? Macro data findings can also result in the deletion of some assumptions. The discussion and sharing of information across diversified groups can eliminate many postulates. In some cases, it may lead to new assumptions. **Any changes should be documented and communicated to the project team.**

Simulation Of A Blank Page

Chapter 11.6

CONSTRUCT THE MODEL

STEPS TO CONDUCTING A SUCCESSFUL SIMULATION PROJECT
1. Formulate And Analyze The Problem
2. Educate The Team On Basic Simulation Principles
3. Develop Model Concept
4. Macro Data Collection
5. Model Concept And Macro Data Review
6. Construct The Model
7. Model Verification
8. Test The Model With Macro Data
9. Model Validation
10. Design Experiments For Evaluating Alternatives
11. Make Multiple Model Runs For Each Alternative
12. Statistical Analysis Of Output
13. Identify Best Solutions And Document Results
14. Presentation Of Results And Implementation

Construct The Model

- Who Builds The Model?

- What Procedures Should Be Followed When Building A Model?

- Are The Variable And Element Names In The Model Documented?

Who Builds The Model?

Many of today's simulation packages make it possible for almost anyone to construct models, but not necessarily credible models. Credible models require a model builder to have **1) a good knowledge of fundamental simulation principles, 2) adequate training and experience with the simulation package being used, and 3) good communication abilities.** Effective model building requires an extensive amount of interaction between a model builder, management, and people providing data to a model. Good verbal skills and patience are assets. Anyone who possesses these characteristics is a candidate for building a model.

Every simulation package has properties and attributes that are unique to that package. The model builder needs to be properly trained on how to apply these features. Most simulation vendors offer some sort of training with their product. The length of the training classes can vary from one to five days. Trainees can learn the basic skills needed to construct models. However, proficiency with any software package is achieved through repetitive use of the package. It is important to give newly trained model builders an opportunity to experiment with a simulation package prior to building his or her first model.

Sometimes the personnel/staff who receive training on a simulation package subsequently leave the position or the company. Their replacement may not be familiar with the simulation package, or simulation in general. Additional training is often by-passed when this occurs. The cost for additional training is usually less than the consequences of not obtaining it. The model building effort can be significantly burdened when a learn-as-you-go type philosophy is employed.

Training provided by simulation vendors is often limited to instructions for operating the features of their respective products. **It is equally important for model builders (and management) to have a basic understanding of simulation methodologies and principles.** This can be accomplished through in-house training, outside consultants, or professors at academic institutions.

What Procedures Should Be Followed When Building A Model?

Today's simulation packages make model building part science and part art. No two people will probably have the same modeling approach. There is never a single right way to model a system, but there are generally some approaches which are better than others. **A good guideline is to build a model section by section. Each section should be functioning properly prior to starting the next.**

A continual interface with operational personnel is vital for establishing model credibility. People who have provided data for a particular section should communicate with the model builder during the construction of that segment. They are the most qualified people for confirming a model's ability to imitate the respective processes associated with their areas. Models of hypothetical systems can involve considerable interfacing with vendors. In these situations, it is equally important to have the vendors actively engaged in the model building process. **A successful** simulation model is the result of a group effort. A model builder should continually promote group ownership throughout the course of a project.

Are The Variable And Element Names In The Model Documented?

Almost every simulation package requires a model builder to give customized names to variables and elements which will be used in a model. Try to assign names that are descriptive of the elements and variables which they are representing. It can make a model much easier to comprehend.

It is also beneficial to document variables and attributes in a dictionary format so anyone can easily determine their purpose. Variable documentation is a standard programming procedure. A model builder might give the name **CTIME** to a variable which represents the cycle time of a certain machine. People other than the model builder may find it difficult to determine that variable's function unless it is documented. This procedure also benefits the model builders. As the number of variables increase, it becomes easier to forget a specific variable's intent.

Chapter 11.7

MODEL VERIFICATION

STEPS TO CONDUCTING A SUCCESSFUL SIMULATION PROJECT

1.	Formulate And Analyze The Problem
2.	Educate The Team On Basic Simulation Principles
3.	Develop Model Concept
4.	Macro Data Collection
5.	Model Concept And Macro Data Review
6.	Construct The Model
7.	Model Verification
8.	Test The Model With Macro Data
9.	Model Validation
10.	Design Experiments For Evaluating Alternatives
11.	Make Multiple Model Runs For Each Alternative
12.	Statistical Analysis Of Output
13.	Identify Best Solutions And Document Results
14.	Presentation Of Results And Implementation

Model Verification

- What Is The Purpose Of Model Verification?

- Can The Model Generate Information Which Can Satisfy The Objectives Of The Study?

- What Techniques Can Be Used To Verify A Model?

What Is The Purpose Of Model Verification?

The primary purpose of model verification is to ascertain the correctness of a model's functional and computational proficiencies. It also affirms that all the macro data has been correctly incorporated into the model. Do the equations and instructions built into a model work as they were intended? Suppose a model element represents a machine that has a normal distribution with a mean time of forty minutes. The cycle time in the model for that machine is verified if the model produces cycle times representative of the normal distribution specified. Any data being sent to external data files needs to be checked to assure its format and correctness.

Can The Model Generate Information Which Will Satisfy The Objectives Of The Study?

Another aim of model verification is to confirm a model's ability to generate output information which can be used to satisfy the objectives of a study. Perhaps an objective is to determine the impact of various lot sizes on product cycle times. Do calculations performed by the model accurately compute statistics which are pertinent to evaluating the effect of lot sizes? The manner in which a simulation package records and presents statistical results can vary from package to package. This is particularly true for simulators. **It is important to understand the context of the information provided in the output reports created by a simulation package**.

What Techniques Can Be Used To Verify A Model?

The verification process does not begin with the completion of building a model. It starts at the onset of a project and remains an on-going task throughout a project. Most simulation packages contain tools for verifying models. They usually consist of debugging and tracing features that permit a model builder to step through various programming statements. Making test runs with selected data known to produce predetermined results is another technique for substantiating the output created by various algorithms and mathematical equations.

The verification effort is usually less time-consuming with packages possessing animation features, than in those that do not. On-screen animation is a good tool for confirming system flows and element functions within a model. Its superior communication capabilities can reduce the time required to verify models. **A good verification technique is to have the model builder confirm the model's construction to an independent party. The independent party is provided with a list of the data and parameters that are supposed to be in the model. He or she then works with the model builder to verify that everything on the list is included in the model**.

Simulation Of A Blank Page

Chapter 11.8

TEST MODEL WITH MACRO DATA

STEPS TO CONDUCTING A SUCCESSFUL SIMULATION PROJECT
1. Formulate And Analyze The Problem
2. Educate The Team On Basic Simulation Principles
3. Develop Model Concept
4. Macro Data Collection
5. Model Concept And Macro Data Review
6. Construct The Model
7. Model Verification
8. Test The Model With Macro Data
9. Model Validation
10. Design Experiments For Evaluating Alternatives
11. Make Multiple Model Runs For Each Alternative
12. Statistical Analysis Of Output
13. Identify Best Solutions And Document Results
14. Presentation Of Results And Implementation

Test The Model With Macro Data

- What Is The Purpose Of Testing A Model With Macro Data?

- What Are Sensitivity Analyses?

- Have The Test Results Been Documented And Communicated To Project Management?

What Is The Purpose Of Testing A Model With Macro Data?

The primary purpose of testing a model with macro data is to determine the input parameters and assumptions that exert the greatest influence on performance criteria. More detailed data may have to be collected for these factors in order to improve the model's ability to imitate the operational characteristics of the system being studied. The goal remains the same: add detail only when necessary.

Valuable insight regarding cause-and-effect relationships between input parameters and performance criteria can be gained with the execution of this step. It helps the project team to focus on areas that will have the greatest impact on system performance. **The potential consequence of by-passing this step is wasted hours investigating factors which have little or no influence on the objectives of a study.**

What Are Sensitivity Analyses?

A procedure frequently used to test the significance of an input parameter is referred to as a **sensitivity analysis**. A sensitivity analysis involves the following steps:

1. **Select an individual input parameter**

2. **Run the model with the parameter's current input values and observe the model's performance with respect to selected criteria**

3. **Increase the value of the selected input parameter**

4. **Make a model run for a specified period of time and observe the results**

5. **Decrease the value of the input parameter and repeat step four (do not change the random number streams)**

6. **Is there a substantial difference in the performance output for the three input values tested? If so, then the input parameter's sensitivity for a performance criterion is noted for the range of the input values used in the test.**

Additional, or more detailed information may have to be collected as a result of sensitivity analyses. Suppose a triangular distribution is the original estimate for an input parameter. A sensitivity analysis then reveals that this parameter significantly influences several performance criteria. Further data collection may be warranted to ensure that the triangular distribution is good representation of the input parameter.

Detailed information may be difficult to obtain for some input parameters. A sensitivity analysis might indicate a need for more precise data, when good data is unattainable. Models of hypothetical systems are especially prone to this condition. Sometimes another simulation model (sometimes referred to as a sub-model or micro-model) can be created in these situations to provide more intricate information about a hypothetical parameter [see Gogg and Sands (1990)].

Have The Tests Results Been Documented And Communicated To Project Management?

It can be beneficial for the model builder (or builders) to keep a record of the tests performed and the ensuing results. Findings should be shared with the project team. **A general consensus needs to be established regarding the test results and the recommended courses of action**. If additional data needs to be collected, then how will it be accomplished, who will do it, and how long will it take? Any major tasks that need to be undertaken as a result of this step should be incorporated into the project schedule. All decisions and actions should be clearly communicated to project management.

Chapter 11.9

MODEL VALIDATION

STEPS TO CONDUCTING A SUCCESSFUL SIMULATION PROJECT
1. Formulate And Analyze The Problem
2. Educate The Team On Basic Simulation Principles
3. Develop Model Concept
4. Macro Data Collection
5. Model Concept And Macro Data Review
6. Construct The Model
7. Model Verification
8. Test The Model With Macro Data
9. Model Validation
10. Design Experiments For Evaluating Alternatives
11. Make Multiple Model Runs For Each Alternative
12. Statistical Analysis Of Output
13. Identify Best Solutions And Document Results
14. Presentation Of Results And Implementation

Model Validation

- Does The Simulation Provide A Reasonable Portrayal Of The System Being Studied?

- What Techniques Can Be Used To Validate Models?

- Have The Stochastics In The Model Been Exercised Sufficiently To See Their Impact?

- Are Changes Needed In The Model?

Does The Simulation Provide A Reasonable Portrayal Of The System Being Studied?

Models often contain a large number of elements, numerous interrelationships, and many rules and logic which govern their interactions. They are typically constructed in a piece-by-piece manner, with each model segment being tested for validity before starting another. **When all segments have been constructed, it is necessary to validate the aggregate behavior of the overall model. How will the model respond when all model segments are working together?**

It is probably fair to say that there are no models of stochastic/dynamic systems, simulation or otherwise, which will provide an exact and perfect imitation of the systems they are representing. Models are just approximations of actual systems. The purpose of model validation is to ensure a model's ability to respond in a manner that is consistent with the rationale and intellect associated with the system being studied. It assures that good judgment and common sense were used when constructing a model.

Model validation establishes credibility in a model. It is especially important for management and other decision-makers to have confidence in the results that will be produced by a model. The validation process, like model verification, really begins at the onset of a project and perseveres throughout its entirety. Keeping the decision-makers actively involved in the model building process will make model validation much simpler.

What Techniques Can Be Used To Validate Models?

Some type of performance data is usually available or attainable from real world systems. Output from a simulation model can be compared to these results when the model is subjected to the same input conditions experienced by the real world system. Standard statistical tests to determine if there is a significant difference between the means of the two outputs can sometimes be performed. These tests generally require larger amounts of data and are more time consuming. Their results are debatable because a model is being hypothesized as being equal to a real system [see Law and Kelton (1990) pages 314-322].

Another approach is to allow system experts to discern the significance of the differences between the outputs. A test related to this approach is called the **Turing Test**. System experts and other knowledgeable people are given copies of real system output and model output. Both outputs are in the same format and their origins are not revealed. The system experts are requested to distinguish between the two. If there are no major differences, the model is considered validated.

Models of hypothetical systems are more difficult to validate. Simulation output can not be compared to actual data when no existing or similar system exists. The best approach in these situations is to have people who are knowledgeable with various aspects of a model to check the simulation inputs and outputs for reasonableness. Sometimes general conclusions can be reached about how a system should respond when different input parameters are changed.

Animation is another feature which can help establish rational validity. Model logistics are easier to grasp in models using animation, than in those without. Animation makes it simpler to explain things and to identify problem areas in a system. It is very useful for rationalizing hypothetical systems. **However, decisions should be based on the statistical analyses of the results produced by simulation.**

Have The Stochastics In The Model Been Exercised Sufficiently To See Their Impact?

Probability distributions are used to generate random behavior in a model. **Has the model run long enough to see the impact of the various distributions?** For example, suppose an exponential distribution is used to represent the repair time for a given equipment failure. The equipment only fails once during each run. These conditions would indicate that the distribution has not been exercised sufficiently to see its impact. The model builder can 1) run the model longer, or 2) reevaluate the use of the exponential distribution as the repair time parameter. Are you more concerned with what would happen if a long repair time was encountered (tail value from the exponential distribution)? If so, then a method which produces a long repair time should be pursued. This could be accomplished with a constant value or a value from a uniform distribution having a range within the repair times under scrutiny.

It is a good practice to incorporate a means within a model to record the values generated from a distribution. Sometimes it is possible to create a dynamic histogram that will reflect those values as the model runs. A visual check can then be made to help determine if the distribution has been exercised sufficiently.

Are Changes Needed In The Model?

Model modifications and replications need to be made until the output reflects a desired level of credibility. Any disparities revealed during model validation should be investigated and understood. **A simulation model responds to the rules and conditions built into it.** The statistical reports and other information created by simulation help educate model users on the cause-and-effect relationships that produce the output responses. Actions for improving model credibility can often be deduced from that data.

The original assumptions made with a model must also be considered when evaluating discrepancies in simulation output. Output can be significantly influenced by assumptions, especially as their numbers and magnitudes increase. Sometimes their impact is not revealed until model validation is attempted. Assumptions may have to be added, deleted, or modified.

Chapter 11.10

DESIGN EXPERIMENTS FOR EVALUATING ALTERNATIVES

STEPS TO CONDUCTING A SUCCESSFUL SIMULATION PROJECT
1. Formulate And Analyze The Problem
2. Educate The Team On Basic Simulation Principles
3. Develop Model Concept
4. Macro Data Collection
5. Model Concept And Macro Data Review
6. Construct The Model
7. Model Verification
8. Test The Model With Macro Data
9. Model Validation
10. Design Experiments For Evaluating Alternatives
11. Make Multiple Model Runs For Each Alternative
12. Statistical Analysis Of Output
13. Identify Best Solutions And Document Results
14. Presentation Of Results And Implementation

Design Experiments For Evaluating Alternatives

- What Alternatives Or Hypotheses Are Being Investigated?

- What Is Experimental Design?

- Factors Factor Levels And Responses

- What Is A Factorial Designed Experiment?

What Alternatives Or Hypotheses Are Being Investigated?

Ideas regarding potential solutions are almost always revealed during the course of building a model. However, it is important to understand that **simulation by itself does not calculate a "best" solution**. It is not an optimizing tool such as linear programming. **The solutions derived from simulation are only as good as the alternatives which are being investigated**. Therefore, prudence must be exercised when selecting candidate solutions.

A simulation study provides information regarding how a system responds to various alternatives and conditions. The responses are totally dependent upon the factors and stipulations built into a model. Effects from multiple factors can be analyzed to determine which factors exert the greatest influence on the performance indexes. This information can be very beneficial for generating candidate solutions.

The alternatives and hypotheses investigated in a simulation study should be directly related to the objectives established for the project. If an objective was to minimize WIP in a manufacturing process, then the design alternatives should investigate solutions for accomplishing that goal.

What Is Experimental Design?

Experimental design is the development of procedures and tests for analyzing and comparing alternatives. Its purpose is to maximize the usefulness of the information produced from simulation runs, while minimizing the effort. Without such a plan, it can be difficult to make an equitable comparison between candidate solutions.

The conditions that produce variability in simulations can be controlled. Stochastic drivers in an experiment can be kept the same for each alternative investigated. An identical sequence of random variates can be produced for each experiment. Variance reduction techniques can be applied to the experiments in order to highlight the contrasts between alternatives. The results produced from the experiments can then be statistically analyzed to evaluate an alternative's performance with respect to selected criteria.

Put in more simple terms, experiments involving stochastics can be designed in a manner that will guarantee that each alternative tested is subjected to the same randomness. Suppose an experiment is planned such that five model replications are to be performed for each of three alternatives. Common random number streams can be used in the respective replications for each alternative. Under these conditions, the differences in the results produced for each alternative can not be attributed to the stochastic conditions experienced in the model replications. Apples are being compared to apples and oranges to oranges.

Decisions regarding experimental design should be clearly communicated to decision-makers and the project team. It is the basis from which conclusions will be drawn.

Factors, Factor Levels, And Responses

Factors are any aspect or condition in a simulation that will be varied from experiment to experiment. A model's input parameters are often used as factors. Factors are hypothesized as having some bearing on the performance of a system. Lot size is an example of a factor that might be investigated in an experiment associated with a manufacturing system.

A factor level is defined as the actual values assigned to a factor in an experiment. Perhaps a lot size of ten is used in one experiment, and a lot size of one is used in another. The factor levels for lot size are ten and one for the respective experiments.

A response is the performance output produced by an experiment. It is the reaction evoked by a stimulus. Suppose multiple factors are being investigated in an experiment, and average product makespan is one of several performance criteria under study. Test results from the experiment indicate an average makespan of two months. We can say that the response of the experiment regarding makespan is two months for the given factors and factor levels.

What Is A Factorial Designed Experiment?

A factorial designed experiment is a method to statistically analyze the effects of multiple factors in an experiment. Factor levels are assigned two values, a high level and a low level. The responses associated with selected performance criteria are observed for all possible combinations of factors and factor levels. Each possible combination is called a design point in an experiment. The number of design points in a factorial experiment is equal to 2^k, where k represents the number of factors. A two-factor experiment will have four design points (2^2). A three factor will have eight (2^3).

Table T11.10A on page 11.10-5 shows a design matrix for a four factor experiment. Each design point would require multiple simulation runs to compute the average responses associated with it. The average responses calculated for each design point can be statistically analyzed to determine the effects elicited by the factors on selected performance criteria (Chapter 11.12, "*Statistical Analyses Of Output*," explains how to statistically analyze response data created from a factorial designed experiment). The effort required to produce the necessary response data increases significantly as the numbers of factors increase. A fractional factorial design can be utilized to reduce this task.

A fractional factorial design utilizes selected design points to analyze the effects of the factors. It is described as a 2^{k-p} factorial designed experiment, where k equals the number of factors and p determines the fractional number of the total design points required. If p equals 1, then one half of the design points are considered (fractional portion of the total design points = $\frac{1}{2^p}$). Which design points should be used is beyond the scope of this book. Additional information on this topic can be found in most text books pertaining to experimental design.

Factorial designed experiments are not mandatory with simulation analyses. They can be advantageous when multiple factors are being examined. The most important point of this model building step is to establish a procedure or plan for comparing simulation results. This plan should include things such as starting conditions, stopping conditions, and the use of random number streams [Smith (1989)].

Factor #	Factor Description	Low Level (-)	High Level (+)
1	Quantity Of Rework Operators	10	12
2	Lot Size	5	10
3	Set-up Time	0.5 hrs	0.8 hrs
4	Pull Strategy	FIFO	By Attribute
5	Workorder Release Schedule	Schedule A	Schedule B

Table T11.10A
Design Matrix For 2^5 Factorial Designed Experiment

The Design matrix tells us the values of the factors that will be used in the model runs for each design point. For example, model runs for Design Point #21 are made with Factor #1 at its high level (12 Rework Operators), Factor #2 at its high level (Lot Size = 10), Factor #3 at its low level (Set-up Time = 0.5 hrs), Factor #4 at its high level (Pull By Attribute), and Factor #5 at its low level (Schedule A).

Design Point	Factor 1	Factor 2	Factor 3	Factor 4	Factor 5
1	+	+	+	+	+
2	−	+	+	+	+
3	+	−	+	+	+
4	−	−	+	+	+
5	+	+	−	+	+
6	−	+	−	+	+
7	+	−	−	+	+
8	−	−	−	+	+
9	+	+	+	−	+
10	−	+	+	−	+
11	+	−	+	−	+
12	−	−	+	−	+
13	+	+	−	−	+
14	−	+	−	−	+
15	+	−	−	−	+
16	−	−	−	−	+
17	+	+	+	+	−
18	−	+	+	+	−
19	+	−	+	+	−
20	−	−	+	+	−
21	+	+	−	+	−
22	−	+	−	+	−
23	+	−	−	+	−
24	−	−	−	+	−
25	+	+	+	−	−
26	−	+	+	−	−
27	+	−	+	−	−
28	−	−	+	−	−
29	+	+	−	−	−
30	−	+	−	−	−
31	+	−	−	−	−
32	−	−	−	−	−

Simulation Of A Blank Page

Chapter 11.11

MAKE MULTIPLE MODEL RUNS FOR EACH ALTERNATIVE

IMPROVE QUALITY & PRODUCTIVITY WITH SIMULATION

STEPS TO CONDUCTING A SUCCESSFUL SIMULATION PROJECT
1. Formulate And Analyze The Problem
2. Educate The Team On Basic Simulation Principles
3. Develop Model Concept
4. Macro Data Collection
5. Model Concept And Macro Data Review
6. Construct The Model
7. Model Verification
8. Test The Model With Macro Data
9. Model Validation
10. Design Experiments For Evaluating Alternatives
11. Make Multiple Model Runs For Each Alternative
12. Statistical Analysis Of Output
13. Identify Best Solutions And Document Results
14. Presentation Of Results And Implementation

Make Multiple Model Runs For Each Alternative

- How Many Model Replications Are Required?

- What Are Antithetic Variates?

- How Can The Length Of A Warm-Up Period Be Determined In A Steady-State Simulation?

- Managing Model Replications And Simulation Output

JMI Consulting Group © 1995

How Many Model Replications Are Required?

Multiple model replications are always required when stochastics are involved. A general rule of thumb is to always perform at least three to five replications for each experiment. A more accurate point estimate is likely to be achieved as the numbers of replications increase. However, **there is a point of diminishing returns where additional model replications will not significantly improve the exactness of a point estimate**. The cost of achieving a desired accuracy level has to be weighed against the cost of attaining it, and the benefits anticipated from it.

There are statistical procedures for calculating the number of model replications needed to establish a confidence level associated with the amount of difference between $\overline{X}(n)$ (a point estimate of a mean) and μ (the theoretical true mean). An α parameter is used to define the probability that the difference between $\overline{X}(n)$ and μ **WILL** exceed a specified amount (the amount of difference or error is designated as **e**). If $\alpha = 0.10$ (10% chance that the difference between $\overline{X}(n)$ and μ **WILL** exceed an amount **e**), then we can be **100 - α** percent confident that the difference between $\overline{X}(n)$ and μ will **NOT** exceed a specified amount **e**. One approach for computing the number of model replications required to ascertain a selected degree of error between $\overline{X}(n)$ and μ is described in Table T11.11A .

Table T11.11A Equation For Calculating Number Of Model Replications

$$N = \left(\frac{t_{n-1,\, 1-\alpha/2}\ S(n)}{e} \right)^{2}$$

N denotes the number of model replications needed to achieve a desired accuracy level

$S(n)$ is a point estimate of σ based on n model replications

e denotes the amount of error between the point estimate $\overline{X}(n)$ and the true mean μ

$t_{n-1,\, 1-\alpha/2}$ is a critical value from a t-distribution with n-1 degrees of freedom

Table T11.11B on page 11.11-4 contains data from ten independent model replications. A point estimate for the average number of parts observed in a queueing buffer is derived from it. Suppose we want to determine the number of model replications needed in this experiment to be **95** percent confident that our point estimate $\overline{X}(n)$ of the average part queue length does not vary from the true mean length μ by more than one part (**e = 1**). Table T11.11C on page 11.11-4 illustrates how this can be accomplished. The calculation indicates a total of **29** replications are required to achieve the accuracy specified.

The results can be interpreted as follows: If the above experiment is repeated 100 times, then we can expect 95 out of the 100 experiments to produce an estimated average queue length

that will not vary from the true mean μ by more than one part. (Keep in mind that an experiment consists of making 29 model replications to calculate a single point estimate for the mean part queue length).

Table T11.11B Point Estimates of μ and σ^2

ith Replication	Average Number of Parts Observed In The Queueing Buffer X_i	$[X_i - \overline{X}(10)]^2$
1	1.96	10.16334
2	8.66	12.33414
3	6.37	1.49328
4	2.12	9.16878
5	5.16	0.00014
6	5.63	0.23232
7	2.20	8.69070
8	5.67	0.27248
9	8.01	8.19104
10	5.70	0.30470
	Total = 51.48	Total = 50.85

$\overline{X}(10) = 51.48/10 = 5.148$ $S^2(10) = 50.85/9 = 5.65$

Table T11.11C Equation For Calculating Number Of Model Replications

$$N = \left(\frac{t_{n-1,\, 1-\alpha/2}\, S(n)}{e} \right)^2 = \left(\frac{2.262 \times 2.38}{1} \right)^2 = 28.9$$

N denotes the number of model replications needed to achieve a desired accuracy level

$S(10)$ is a point estimate of σ based on 10 model replications $= \sqrt{5.65} = 2.38$

e denotes the amount of error between the point estimate $\overline{X}(10)$ and the true mean μ

$t_{10-1,\, 1-.05/2}$ is a critical value from a t-distribution with 9 degrees of freedom

If you need further clarification about the principle of a confidence interval, you can work through the following exercise.

Let's assume that the numbers in the following table are representative of all the possible output responses that might be produced from an independent model replication. The theoretical true mean μ of the distribution of all possible outcomes is **30.64** and the variance σ^2 is **52.55**.

21	21	22	22	22	22	23	23	23	23
23	23	24	24	24	24	24	25	25	25
25	25	25	25	26	26	26	26	26	26
26	27	27	27	27	27	27	27	27	28
28	28	28	28	28	28	28	28	28	29
29	29	29	29	29	29	30	30	30	30
31	31	31	31	31	31	32	33	33	33
33	33	33	34	34	34	34	34	35	35
35	36	36	36	37	38	39	39	40	40
41	41	42	42	45	46	47	52	54	58

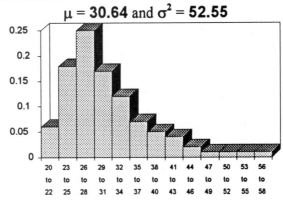

Theoretical Distribution Of All Possible Outcomes
$\mu = $ **30.64** and $\sigma^2 = $ **52.55**

The principle of a confidence interval associated with the number of model replications needed to ascertain the accuracy of a point estimate of μ can be demonstrated by utilizing the numbers in the previous table with the following exercise:

Step 1 - Make 100 small squares of paper and copy each number from the above table onto each square of paper.

Step 2 - Put the paper squares into a container.

Step 3 - Reach into the container and randomly extract a square of paper. This is representative of making an independent model replication.

Step 4 - Record the number shown on the selected square of paper.

Step 5 - Return the selected square of paper to the container and repeat steps 3 and 4 an additional five times.

Step 6 - Calculate a point estimate of σ from the six values recorded.

For this example lets assume the following values are extracted: **42,34,27,35,23** and **36**. Our point estimate of σ is **S(6) = 6.79**.

Step 7 - Calculate the number of model replications needed to be **90%** confident that $\overline{X}(n)$ does not differ from μ by more that **5**.

$$N = \left(\frac{t_{n-1,\, 1-\alpha/2}\ S(n)}{e} \right)^2 = \left(\frac{2.015 \times 6.79}{5} \right)^2 = 7.48 \cong 8$$

For this example eight model replications will be required.

The critical **t** value from a t-distribution for a **90%** confidence level and **5** degrees of freedom is **2.015**

Step 8 - Reach into the container and randomly extract a square of paper. This is representative of making an independent model replication.

Step 9 - Record the number shown on the selected square of paper.

Step 10 - Return the selected square of paper to the container and repeat steps 8 and 9 an additional seven times.

Step 11 - Calculate a point estimate of μ from the eight values recorded.

If we perform steps eight through eleven **100** times, then we can expect **90** of the point estimates for μ (μ = **30.64** for this example) not to differ from μ by more than **5**. The results from ten repetitions of this exercise can be seen in the following table.

REP	Random Sample Values	$\overline{X}(8)$	$\overline{X}(8)$ Within Error Limits ± 5 From μ ?
1	33, 29, 24, 25, 26, 38, 25, 24	28.00	YES
2	27, 39, 31, 41, 26, 28, 46, 39	34.65	YES
3	51, 36, 28, 45, 33, 26, 27, 29	34.37	YES
4	25, 24, 28, 30, 24 ,21, 34, 29	26.87	YES
5	34, 24, 21, 30, 29, 27, 24,36	28.12	YES
6	26, 23, 26, 30, 55, 32, 29, 28	31.12	YES
7	28, 26, 35, 44, 31, 50, 27,23	33.00	YES
8	41, 24, 31, 57 , 21, 23, 28,56	34.12	YES
9	20, 27, 31, 26, 21 ,25, 24,30	25.50	NO
10	27, 21, 33, 46, 33, 36, 20,50	33.25	YES

What Are Antithetic Variates?

Antithetic variates are random outcomes produced from the complementary values of the decimal numbers in a random number stream (e.g., The antithetic decimal number of **0.21235** is calculated as **1 - 0.21235** or **0.78765**). They are used with simulation as a variance reduction technique. Paired-runs are made for each model replication. Ordinary random number streams are utilized to create stochastic variates (random values extracted from a probability distribution) in the first run. The second run produces stochastic variates from the antithetic numbers of the decimal random numbers used in the first run. The output responses from the two runs (non-antithetic and antithetic) are then averaged. The combined average response represents the output for a single model replication.

Recall that a random number stream contains an unpredictable sequence of decimal numbers with values between **0** and **1**. Since chance is being imitated, there is a possibility that the estimated average response calculated from a limited number of model replications may show considerable partiality towards one side of its true mean. Duplicating a model run using antithetic number streams should produce a response that favors the opposite side. A point estimate for a mean response calculated from the combined average of the two results (non-antithetic and antithetic) can provide a better estimate of the true mean.

Table T11.11D Using Antithetic Number Streams

RN_i = Decimal random number generated from the random number stream selected for use with the ith model replication
$V1_i$ = ln $(1-RN_i)$ (-10) Random value extracted from Exponential Distribution using RN_i
AN_i = $1 - RN_i$ Antithetic decimal random number derived from RN_i
$V2_i$ = ln $(1-AN_i)$ (-10) Random value extracted from Exponential Distribution using AN_i
AVG_i = $(V1_i + V1_i) + 2$ Average response derived from the paired responses $V1_i$ and $V2_i$

ith Model Rep	RN_i	$V1_i$	AN_i	$V2_i$	AVG_i
1,	0.12855	1.376	0.87145	20.514	10.945
2	0.37437	4.690	0.62563	9.825	7.258
3	0.13972	1.505	0.86028	19.681	10.593
4	0.48056	6.550	0.51944	7.328	6.939
5	0.06705	0.694	0.93295	27.023	13.859
6	0.05029	0.516	0.94971	29.899	15.208
7	0.21235	2.387	0.78765	15.495	8.941
8	0.27942	3.277	0.72058	12.750	8.041
9	0.11733	1.248	0.88267	21.428	11.338
10	0.37998	4.780	0.62002	9.676	7.228
		$\sum_{i=1}^{10} V1_i = 27.02$		$\sum_{i=1}^{10} V2_i = 173.62$	$\sum_{i=1}^{10} AVG_i = 100.32$

Table T11.11D contains a simple example which illustrates the motivation for using antithetic number streams. Consider an experiment that consists of ten model replications. Each replication involves obtaining a random value from an exponential distribution with a mean value of **10**. A unique random number stream is used with each replication to generate a single random decimal number from which an exponential value (response) is calculated. The computed responses from the ten replications are then summed and averaged to estimate the distribution's true mean. The resulting point estimate for the distribution's true mean is **2.70**. It is significantly less than **10**.

Ten additional model replications are then performed using the antithetic numbers of the decimal numbers used in the previous replications. The ensuing point estimate of the distribution's mean is now **17.4**. This is substantially higher than the true mean. The last column in the table shows the combined average of the responses obtained from the original random numbers and their antithetic values. The point estimate of the mean **(10.03)** derived from the combined averages is very close to the true mean.

How Can The Length Of A Warm-Up Period Be Determined In A Steady-State Simulation?

A steady-state condition implies that a simulation has reached a point in time where the state of the simulation is independent of the initial start-up conditions. The amount of time required to achieve steady-state conditions is referred to as a warm-up period. Data collection begins after a warm-up period is completed. <u>Determining the length of a warm-up period can be accomplished by utilizing moving averages calculated from the output produced from multiple model replications</u>. One such procedure for accomplishing this is called the Welch graphical method [Law and Kelton (1991) pages 545-551].

Suppose a simulation model is constructed to analyze the monthly WIP (Work In Progress) costs associated with a given system design. Five independent model replications are then made. Each run records the monthly WIP costs incurred for every month over a **39** month period. Table T11.11F on page 11.11-9 displays the results observed for each model replication. The average WIP costs for the **ith** period are then calculated across all **(j=5)** model replications. Column six displays the averaged results. Graph G11.11A on page 11.11-10 presents a graphical representation of the results.

<u>A steady-state condition occurs at a point where the curve of the transient mean flattens out</u>. Graph G11.11A does not level out. It is not possible to visually determine when and if a steady-state condition is achieved. Graphs that plot a moving average for each period are more likely to flatten out. A moving average cost for each period can be derived according to the equation shown in Table T11.11E where $\overline{Y}_i(w)$ represents the computed moving average for the ith period..

Table T11.11E Calculating Moving Averages	
$$\overline{Y}_i(w) = \begin{cases} \sum_{s=-w}^{w} \dfrac{\overline{Y}_{i+s}}{2w+1} & \text{for } i = w+1,...,m-w \\ \sum_{s=-(i-1)}^{i-1} \dfrac{\overline{Y}_{i+s}}{2i-1} & \text{for } i = 1,...,w \end{cases}$$	**m** denotes the total number of periods in each model replication **w** represents the "window" of the moving average. If $i \le w$, then the value of the current period is averaged with the values from the (i-1) preceding periods and the (i-1) following periods. If $i > w$, then the value of the current period is averaged with the values from the **w** preceding periods and the **w** following periods. **Note:** The value of m must be chosen to be large, and w must be less than or equal to **m/2**

Table T11.11F Determining A Warm-Up Period In A Steady-State Simulation

$$\bar{Y}_3(5) = \frac{422.00 + 468.16 + 676.45 + 572.88 + 374.10}{5} = 502.72$$

$$\bar{Y}_{10}(5) = \frac{374.10 + 842.90 + 625.92 + 473.08 + 685.88 + 528.79 + 500.22 + 716.52 + 443.33 + 487.13 + 800.55}{11} = 588.95$$

ith Period	Y_{ij} = Observed Cost During ith Period And jth Model Replication (All Costs In Thousand Of Dollars)					Average Cost Per Period	$\bar{Y}_i(w)$ Moving Average Cost During ith Period For Various Values Of w		
Period	Rep1	Rep2	Rep3	Rep4	Rep5	$\bar{Y}_i$	w=5	w=10	w=19
1	465.18	224.24	279.99	596.05	544.54	422.00	422.00	422.00	422.00
2	521.58	357.41	358.01	872.99	230.81	468.16	522.20	522.20	522.20
3	663.02	407.14	532.68	244.39	1535.00	676.45	502.72	502.72	502.72
4	389.93	495.02	296.21	240.45	1442.82	572.88	568.92	568.92	568.92
5	240.74	737.54	318.34	286.13	287.77	374.10	571.26	571.26	571.26
6	461.24	1085.18	776.97	565.59	1325.52	842.90	560.94	560.94	560.94
7	461.64	352.09	241.88	1051.51	1022.49	625.92	587.72	563.86	563.86
8	1184.09	308.75	263.12	286.97	322.46	473.08	585.46	574.53	574.53
9	1276.80	202.80	727.65	643.93	578.21	685.88	568.25	569.68	569.68
10	473.76	460.59	325.86	906.02	477.74	528.79	588.95	578.06	578.06
11	405.50	405.23	503.67	697.96	488.75	500.22	611.93	565.67	565.67
12	1161.52	284.69	352.24	867.54	916.62	716.52	575.28	568.46	558.81
13	376.81	500.97	192.96	509.00	636.91	443.33	546.57	569.65	561.05
14	352.05	329.30	587.45	636.11	530.74	487.13	593.43	564.58	563.82
15	518.96	634.81	416.81	533.05	1899.13	800.55	588.58	566.04	560.68
16	673.88	852.97	563.86	179.72	864.17	626.92	564.45	582.64	558.51
17	376.99	1048.67	290.92	205.43	276.93	439.79	562.67	565.07	567.40
18	139.26	339.08	563.49	319.10	189.20	310.03	542.35	557.70	563.35
19	199.54	4032.35	355.94	138.88	215.99	988.54	553.87	562.11	560.86
20	542.79	908.45	633.90	349.55	727.93	632.52	564.45	552.18	561.87
21	383.47	317.29	165.11	345.11	106.20	263.44	557.38	554.46	
22	276.26	387.05	336.19	789.89	613.58	480.59	543.47	554.19	
23	336.39	388.63	605.87	315.20	818.90	493.00	546.31	563.67	
24	562.06	323.83	1311.94	339.76	312.95	570.11	569.55	559.60	
25	931.46	236.80	706.43	484.30	658.11	603.42	523.10	566.66	
26	182.82	352.79	991.44	271.73	1815.32	722.82	518.01	549.41	
27	589.21	649.52	544.64	296.36	289.96	473.94	539.02	547.96	
28	103.42	936.04	393.21	771.45	151.18	471.06	578.57	567.48	
29	219.14	1338.29	163.15	169.59	938.19	565.67	566.28	567.54	
30	169.36	841.89	651.41	492.09	232.72	477.50	572.21		
31	791.25	139.11	734.38	807.81	410.16	576.54	557.21		
32	1360.99	274.57	457.19	148.87	231.46	494.62	545.72		
33	530.04	1259.50	497.51	1300.90	990.27	915.64	579.87		
34	198.98	275.20	177.60	723.29	414.02	357.82	565.35		
35	523.28	1012.45	904.77	212.75	523.06	635.26			
36	633.30	723.07	431.72	245.69	158.22	438.40			
37	631.47	455.12	1256.28	287.57	351.78	596.44			
38	807.24	1627.84	994.43	215.50	603.36	849.67			
39	271.41	138.54	352.43	441.73	352.38	311.30			

Graphs G11.11B through G11.11D on page 11.11-10 plot the moving average WIP costs for **w=5**, **w=10**, and **w=19** respectively. The curve for **w=19** is selected for estimating the warm-up period **p** because it is the flatter of the three graphs. After twelve periods, the curve appears to be relatively flat. A regression analysis could be performed to validate that assumption. For this example, we will assume it is sufficiently flat and select a warm-up period of **p=12.**

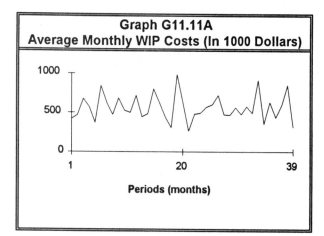

Graph G11.11A
Average Monthly WIP Costs (In 1000 Dollars)

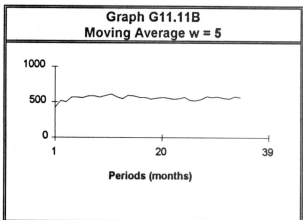

Graph G11.11B
Moving Average w = 5

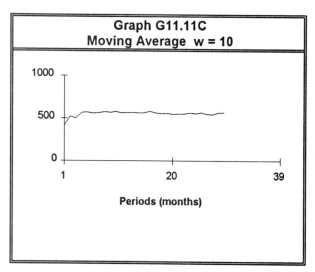

Graph G11.11C
Moving Average w = 10

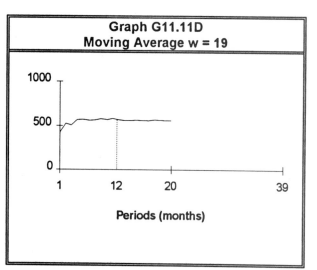

Graph G11.11D
Moving Average w = 19

Managing Model Replications And Simulation Output

Each model replication is performed under a certain set of conditions. It is wise to record these conditions in a journal for future references. Things such as random number streams selected, model run time, factor levels, and model filename should be noted. The latter is important when a separate model is created for individual model replications.

Results generated from model replications are often written to external data files for analyses with other software packages. The contents of such files should be documented. It is easy to forget a data file's purpose when there is no documentation regarding its contents.

Chapter 11.12

STATISTICAL ANALYSIS OF OUTPUT

STEPS TO CONDUCTING A SUCCESSFUL SIMULATION PROJECT
1. Formulate And Analyze The Problem
2. Educate The Team On Basic Simulation Principles
3. Develop Model Concept
4. Macro Data Collection
5. Model Concept And Macro Data Review
6. Construct The Model
7. Model Verification
8. Test The Model With Macro Data
9. Model Validation
10. Design Experiments For Evaluating Alternatives
11. Make Multiple Model Runs For Each Alternative
12. Statistical Analysis Of Output
13. Identify Best Solutions And Document Results
14. Presentation Of Results And Implementation

Statistical Analysis Of Output

- **Confidence Intervals For Terminating And Steady-State Simulations**

- **Comparing And Evaluating Alternatives**

- **Analyzing Factorial Designed Experiments**

Confidence Intervals For Terminating And Steady-State Simulations

Confidence intervals for point estimates of μ associated with terminating simulations are described in chapter 9, "*Statistical Analyses Of Simulation Output*." We can conclude from that information that there are three ingredients needed for constructing a confidence interval: **1) a point estimate of a sample's mean parameter, 2) a point estimate of a sample's variance, and 3) a critical t-value derived from a Student's t- distribution.** The statistical equations associated with each ingredient are as follows:

$$1.\ \overline{X}(n) = \frac{\sum_{i=1}^{n} X_i}{n} \quad 2.\ S^2(n) = \frac{\sum_{i=1}^{n} \left[X_i - \overline{X}(n) \right]^2}{n-1} \quad 3.\ t_{n-1,1-\alpha/2}$$

The equation for calculating a confidence interval is as follows:

$$\overline{X}(n) \pm t_{n-1,\ 1-\alpha/2} \sqrt{\frac{S^2(n)}{n}}$$

Table T9D on page 9-8 illustrates the application of this equation to establish a confidence interval for the data presented in Table T9C on page 9-7. The results tell us that we can be **90%** confident that the true mean for the average number of parts in the queueing buffer is contained within the interval **[0.23, 2.71]**.

Confidence intervals for steady-state simulations can be produced in a similar fashion. In a steady-state simulation, output generated from a single model replication consists of selected response values observed over repetitive time periods. An overall average response for each replication must first be determined in order to establish a value for $\overline{X}(n)$. This is accomplished by summing all responses occurring in a model replication starting at period **p+1** (**p** is the warm-up period) and ending at period **m** (the total number of periods in a replication). The result is then divided by the total number of periods summed (**m-p**) to obtain the average response per model replication. The mathematical equation for accomplishing this is shown below.

$$\overline{Y}_i(m,p) = \frac{\sum_{j=p+1}^{m} Y_{ij}}{m-p}$$

m represents the total number of periods in a model replication
p = number of periods in the warm-up period
$\overline{Y}_i(m,p)$ = average response in the ith model replication from period **p+1** to **m**
Yij = response in the ith model replication and jth period

Table T11.12A utilizes this equation to calculate a confidence interval for the monthly WIP cost data in Table T11.11F. Data from periods **13** through **39** are used in the calculations because a warm-up interval of **12** periods is chosen. The average response for each model replication is shown at the bottom of each data column. The point estimate for the steady-state mean response for the monthly WIP cost is **$556520**. A **90%** confidence interval is **[$400646, $712392]**.

Table T11.12A

ith Period	Y_{ij} = Observed Cost During ith Period And jth Model Replication (All Costs In Thousand Of Dollars)				
Period	Rep1	Rep2	Rep3	Rep4	Rep5
13	376.81	500.97	192.96	509.00	636.91
14	352.05	329.30	587.45	636.11	530.74
15	518.96	634.81	416.81	533.05	1899.13
16	673.88	852.97	563.86	179.72	864.17
17	376.99	1048.67	290.92	205.43	276.93
18	139.26	339.08	563.49	319.10	189.20
19	199.54	4032.35	355.94	138.88	215.99
20	542.79	908.45	633.90	349.55	727.93
21	383.47	317.29	165.11	345.11	106.20
22	276.26	387.05	336.19	789.89	613.58
23	336.39	388.63	605.87	315.20	818.90
24	562.06	323.83	1311.94	339.76	312.95
25	931.46	236.80	706.43	484.30	658.11
26	182.82	352.79	991.44	271.73	1815.32
27	589.21	649.52	544.64	296.36	289.96
28	103.42	936.04	393.21	771.45	151.18
29	219.14	1338.29	163.15	169.59	938.19
30	169.36	841.89	651.41	492.09	232.72
31	791.25	139.11	734.38	807.81	410.16
32	1360.99	274.57	457.19	148.87	231.46
33	530.04	1259.50	497.51	1300.90	990.27
34	198.98	275.20	177.60	723.29	414.02
35	523.28	1012.45	904.77	212.75	523.06
36	633.30	723.07	431.72	245.69	158.22
37	631.47	455.12	1256.28	287.57	351.78
38	807.24	1627.84	994.43	215.50	603.36
39	271.41	138.54	352.43	441.73	352.38
$\overline{Y}_i(m,p) = \dfrac{\sum_{j=p+1}^{m} Y_{ij}}{m-p} =$	469.70	752.74	565.96	427.05	567.14

1. Point Estimate Of Steady-State Mean

$$\overline{X}(n) = \sum_{i=1}^{n} \frac{\overline{Y}_i(m,p)}{n}$$

$$\overline{X}(5) = \sum_{i=1}^{5} \frac{\overline{Y}_i(39,12)}{5}$$

$$\overline{X}(5) = \frac{469.70 + 752.74 + 565.96 + 427.05 + 567.14}{5}$$

$$\overline{X}(5) = 556.52$$

2. Point Estimate Of Variance

$$S^2(n) = \sum_{i=1}^{n} \frac{[Y(m,p) - X(n)]^2}{n-1}$$

$$S^2(5) = 15752.76$$

3. Critical t-value From t-distribution

95% Confidence

$$t_{4,0.975} = 2.776$$

4. Confidence Interval Calculation

$$X(5) \pm t_{4,0.975} \sqrt{\frac{S^2(5)}{5}}$$

$$556.52 \pm 2.776 \sqrt{\frac{15752.76}{5}}$$

$$556.52 \pm 2.776 \times 56.129$$

$$[400.646, 712.392]$$

Comparing And Evaluating Alternatives

Simulation analyses can involve the comparison of two design configurations, or two alternatives. The goal is to determine 1) Is one alternative better than another with respect to a selected performance criterion?, and 2) If one is superior, then how much better is it? There are two statistical tests that can help answer these questions. They are 1) a **Paired-t test**, and 2) a **Two-sample test.** Both involve making point estimates of the average difference between the mean responses for two design configurations. The results of these tests provide information for constructing a confidence interval for a point estimate of the mean difference.

A Paired-t test requires the number of model replications performed for each alternative to be equal. It is also employed when common random number streams are used in the respective model replications. The equation for calculating a confidence interval under these conditions is displayed below.

$$\bar{d} - t_{n-1,\,1-\alpha/2}\sqrt{\frac{S_d^{\,2}}{n}} < \mu_d < \bar{d} + t_{n-1,\,1-\alpha/2}\sqrt{\frac{S_d^{\,2}}{n}}$$

$$\text{where} \quad S_d^{\,2} = \frac{n\sum_{i=1}^{n} d_i^{\,2} - \left(\sum_{i=1}^{n} d_i\right)^2}{n(n-1)}$$

n represents the number of paired observations (independent model replications)

X_{1i} represents the response observed for design configuration #1 on the **ith** model replication

X_{2i} represents the response observed for design configuration #2 on the **ith** model replication

d_i is the difference between X_{1i} - X_{2i} in the **ith** model replication

$S_d^{\,2}$ represents a point estimate of the variance between the differences

Suppose terminating simulations are being used to analyze labor utilization for two alternatives. Let's call the two alternatives **Method #1** and **Method #2**. Ten model replications are performed for each alternative. Common random number streams are used with each set of replications. Table T11.12B on page 11.12-6 contains labor utilization data (expressed in percent of total work time) generated from each model replication. A **90** percent confidence interval for the difference in the labor utilizations for the two methods is **[-1.63, 7.23]**. In other words, we can be **90%** confident that the true difference between the labor utilizations in **Methods #1** and **#2** is contained within the interval **-1.63** to **7.23**.

$$\bar{d} - t_{n-1,\,1-\alpha/2}\sqrt{\frac{S_d^{\,2}}{n}} < \mu_d < \bar{d} + t_{n-1,\,1-\alpha/2}\sqrt{\frac{S_d^{\,2}}{n}}$$

$$2.8 - 1.833\sqrt{\frac{58.4}{10}} < \mu_d < 2.8 + 1.833\sqrt{\frac{58.4}{10}}$$

$$-1.63 < \mu_d < 7.23$$

For this example, the true difference μ_d has the possibility of being equal to **0**. A value of **0** implies that there is no difference between **Method #1** and **Method #2**. Therefore, we can not conclude that one method is superior to the other regarding labor utilization.

Table T11.12B
Confidence Interval For Estimating The Difference Between Two Means

Paired Observations	Labor Utilization (%) In The ith Model Replication For Method #1	Labor Utilization (%) In The ith Model Replication For Method #1	Difference Between Methods #1 and #2 on the ith Model Replication	Square Of The Difference On the ith Model Replication
Replication i	X_{1i}	X_{2i}	$d_i - X_{1i} - X_{2i}$	d_i^2
1	75	67	8	64
2	76	85	-9	81
3	73	68	5	25
4	74	62	12	144
5	76	71	5	25
6	91	87	4	16
7	55	63	-8	64
8	67	55	12	144
9	85	90	-5	25
10	89	85	4	16
			$\sum_{i=1}^{10} d_i = 28$	$\sum_{i=1}^{10} d_i^2 = 604$

$$S_d^2 = \frac{n \sum_{i=1}^{n} d_i^2 - \left(\sum_{i=1}^{n} d_i\right)^2}{n(n-1)}$$

$$\overline{d} - t_{n-1,\,1-\alpha/2} \sqrt{\frac{S_d^2}{n}} < \mu_d < \overline{d} + t_{n-1,\,1-\alpha/2} \sqrt{\frac{S_d^2}{n}}$$

$$S_d^2 = \frac{10 \sum_{i=1}^{10} d_i^2 - \left(\sum_{i=1}^{10} d_i\right)^2}{10(9)}$$

$$2.8 - 1.833 \sqrt{\frac{58.4}{10}} < \mu_d < 2.8 + 1.833 \sqrt{\frac{58.4}{10}}$$

$$S_d^2 = \frac{10(604) - (28)^2}{90} = 58.4$$

$$-1.63 < \mu_d < 7.23$$

A **Two-sample test** is another means of testing the difference between two means. **It is employed when one or both of the following conditions exist: 1) the number of model replications is not equal for the two alternatives being compared, and 2) common random number streams are not used when simulating both alternatives**. The equation for constructing a confidence interval with this test is displayed on the following page.

Suppose in the previous example that **15** model replications are performed for another alternative, **Method #3**, and each replication is independent of the **10** replications performed for **Method #1** (i.e., common random number streams are not used for both methods). Table T11.12C on page 11.12-7 contains labor utilization data produced for this scenario. A **90%** confidence interval for the difference in the labor utilizations between **Method #1** and **Method #3** is **[-12.25%, -5.41%]**.

Equation For Two-Sample Test

$$\left(\overline{X}_1(n_1) - \overline{X}_2(n_2)\right) - t_{v,\,1-\alpha/2}\sqrt{\frac{S_1^{\,2}(n_1)}{n_1} + \frac{S_2^{\,2}(n_2)}{n_2}} < \mu_1 - \mu_2 < \left(\overline{X}_1(n_1) - \overline{X}_2(n_2)\right) + t_{v,\,1-\alpha/2}\sqrt{\frac{S_1^{\,2}(n_1)}{n_1} + \frac{S_2^{\,2}(n_2)}{n_2}}$$

n_1, n_2 represent the number of model replications for alternatives #1 and #2

$\overline{X}_1(n_1), \overline{X}_2(n_2)$ represent the respective point estimates for the mean response of alternatives #1 and #2

$S_1^{\,2}(n_1), S_2^{\,2}(n_2)$ represent the respective point estimates for the variance of alternative #1 and #2

$t_{v,\,1-\alpha/2}$ represents a value from the t-distribution with v degrees of freedom

v is estimated as follows:

$$v \cong \frac{\left(S_1^{\,2}(n_1)/n_1 + S_2^{\,2}(n_2)/n_2\right)^2}{\dfrac{\left(S_1^{\,2}(n_1)/n_1\right)^2}{n_1-1} + \dfrac{\left(S_2^{\,2}(n_2)/n_2\right)^2}{n_2-1}}$$

Table T11.12C Two-Sample Test

ith Model Rep	Method #1			Method #2		
	Labor Utilization (%) In The ith Model Replication For Method #1 X_{1i}	$X_{1i} - \overline{X}(n_1)$	$\left(X_{1i} - \overline{X}(n_1)\right)^2$	Labor Utilization (%) In The ith Model Replication For Method #1 X_{2i}	$X_{2i} - \overline{X}(n_2)$	$\left(X_{2i} - \overline{X}(n_2)\right)^2$
1	77	-3.7	13.69	89	-0.53	0.28
2	82	1.3	1.69	91	1.47	2.16
3	89	8.3	68.89	91	1.47	2.16
4	76	-4.7	22.09	88	-1.53	2.34
5	86	5.3	28.09	88	-1.53	2.34
6	76	-4.7	22.09	87	-2.53	6.40
7	77	-3.7	13.69	88	-1.53	2.34
8	84	3.3	10.89	89	-0.53	0.28
9	88	7.3	53.29	90	-0.47	0.22
10	72	-8.7	75.69	91	1.47	2.16
11				90	0.47	0.22
12				91	1.47	2.16
13				89	-0.53	0.28
14				91	1.47	2.16
15				90	0.47	0.22
	$\sum_{i=1}^{10} X_{1i} = 807$		$\sum_{i=1}^{10}\left(X_{1i} - \overline{X}(n_1)\right)^2 = 310.$	$\sum_{i=1}^{15} X_{2i} = 1343$		$\sum_{i=1}^{15}\left(X_{2i} - \overline{X}(n_2)\right)^2 = 25.72$

$$\overline{X}_1(n_1) = \frac{\sum_{i=1}^{n_1} X_{1i}}{n_1} = \overline{X}_1(10) = \frac{807}{10} = 80.7 \qquad S_1^{\,2}(n_1) = \frac{\sum_{i=1}^{n_1}[X_{1i} - \overline{X}(n_1)]^2}{n_1 - 1} = \frac{310.1}{9} = 34.45$$

$$\overline{X}_2(n_2) = \frac{\sum_{i=1}^{n_2} X_{2i}}{n_1} = \overline{X}_2(15) = \frac{1343}{15} = 89.53 \qquad S_2^{\,2}(n_2) = \frac{\sum_{i=1}^{n_2}[X_{2i} - \overline{X}(n_2)]^2}{n_2 - 1} = \frac{25.72}{14} = 1.837$$

$$v \cong \frac{(34.45/10 + 1.837/15)^2}{\dfrac{(34.45/10)^2}{9} + \dfrac{(1.837/15)^2}{14}} \cong 10$$

$$-8.83 - 1.81\sqrt{\frac{34.45}{10} + \frac{1.837}{15}} < \mu_1 - \mu_2 < -8.83 + 1.81\sqrt{\frac{34.45}{10} + \frac{1.837}{15}}$$

$$-12.25 < \mu_1 - \mu_2 < -5.41$$

Analyzing Factorial Designed Experiments

Sometimes simulation analyses are used to determine the effects that various factors exert on selected performance criteria. Factorial designed experiments are one means of providing this type of information. The results produced from these experiments can be statistically analyzed to measure the 1) main effects, and 2) interactive effects that selected factors exert on performance indices (system responses).

__A main effect__ (denoted E_1) is the average change in a response resulting from raising the ith factor from a specified low level to a specified high level. Suppose we perform a simulation to investigate three factors (lot size, set-up time, and quantity of machines) regarding their individual effects on a product's makespan. A factorial designed experiment can be used to analyze their effects.

A design matrix is constructed according to the procedures described in chapter 11.11, "__*Design Experiments For Evaluating Alternatives*__." The resulting matrix is reflected in Table T11.12D on page 11.12-9. High and low levels selected for each factor are also illustrated. The average makespan response observed after performing a single model replication for each design point is displayed in the fifth column of the table. Common random number streams are used with each model replication for each design point. The main effect of raising each factor from its low to high level can be calculated with the following equations, where R_i is the response observed in the ith design point.

Main Effect Factor #1
$$E_1 = \frac{+R_1 - R_2 + R_3 - R_4 + R_5 - R_6 + R_7 - R_8}{2^{K-1}}$$

Main Effect Factor #2
$$E_2 = \frac{+R_1 + R_2 - R_3 - R_4 + R_5 + R_6 - R_7 - R_8}{2^{K-1}}$$

Main Effect Factor #3
$$E_3 = \frac{+R_1 + R_2 + R_3 + R_4 - R_5 - R_6 - R_7 - R_8}{2^{K-1}}$$

Notice the manner in which the main effects are computed. The signs (**+ or -**) in each factor column are attached to the respective response for each design point. The ensuing outcomes are then summed to determine the main effects. The main effect of raising lot size from **5** to **10** (denoted E_1) is to increase product makespan an average of **0.8** days per part. Adding an additional machine (denoted E_2) decreased the makespan by an average of **6.3** days. Decreasing the rework rate from **12%** to **6%** (denoted E_3) suggests that the product makespan is not affected by the reduction.

An __interactive effect__ tells us if the effect of a given factor is influenced by the level of another factor. If there is a significant interactive effect, then we can not be certain that a main effect is due solely to the raising or lowering of a factor level. These effects (denoted E_{12}, E_{13}, E_{23}) can be computed with the equations displayed on page 11.12-9.

Interactive Effect Factors #1 And #2

$$E_{12} = \frac{+R_1 - R_2 - R_3 + R_4 + R_5 - R_6 - R_7 + R_8}{2^{K-1}}$$

Interactive Effect Factors #1 And #3

$$E_{13} = \frac{+R_1 - R_2 + R_3 - R_4 - R_5 + R_6 - R_7 + R_8}{2^{K-1}}$$

Interactive Effect Factors #2 And #3

$$E_{23} = \frac{+R_1 + R_2 - R_3 - R_4 - R_5 - R_6 + R_7 + R_8}{2^{K-1}}$$

The sign (**+ or -**) given to the responses in each calculation can be derived from the design matrix. Consider the sign given to the response of the second design point (R_2) in the calculation of (E_{13}). It is negative (**-**). The negative is derived from looking at the sign in the design matrix for **Design Point #2, Factor #1**; and **Design Point #2, Factor #3**. The respective values are + and -. Like signs (+,+ or -,-) result in a positive sign being attached to the design point response. Opposite signs, (-,+ or +,-), result in a negative sign.

Factor	Low Level (-)	High Level (+)
1. Lot Size	5	10
2. Machine Quantity	1	2
3. Rework Rate	6%	12%

Table T11.12D Makespan Responses (In Days) For Factorial Designed Experiment

R_1 represents the makespan response (the time required to manufacture a product) observed for the model replication made for **Design Point #1**. Lot Size At High Level (10), Machine Quantity At High Level (2), and Rework Rate At High Level (12%)

Design Point	Factor #1 Level (Lot Size)	Factor #2 Level (Machine Quantity)	Factor #3 Level (Rework Rate)	Response
1	+	+	+	R_1 = 5.7
2	–	+	+	R_2 = 5.0
3	+	–	+	R_3 = 12.1
4	–	–	+	R_4 = 11.1
5	+	+	–	R_5 = 5.7
6	–	+	–	R_6 = 5.0
7	+	–	–	R_7 = 12.1
8	–	–	–	R_8 = 11.1

Calculating "Main" And "Interactive" Effects From Data In Table T11.12D

MAIN EFFECTS

Lot Size E_1

$$E_1 = \frac{+5.7 - 5.0 + 12.1 - 11.1 + 5.7 - 5.0 + 12.1 - 11.1}{4} = 0.8$$

Machine Quantity E_2

$$E_2 = \frac{+5.7 + 5.0 - 12.1 - 11.1 + 5.7 + 5.0 - 12.1 - 11.1}{4} = -6.3$$

Rework Rate E_3

$$E_3 = \frac{+5.7 + 5.0 + 12.1 + 11.1 - 5.7 - 5.0 - 12.1 - 11.1}{4} = 0.0$$

INTERACTIVE EFFECTS

Lot Size & Machine Quantity E_{12}

$$E_{12} = \frac{+5.7 - 5.0 - 12.1 + 11.1 + 5.7 - 5.0 - 12.1 + 11.1}{4} = -0.2$$

Lot Size & Rework Rate E_{13}

$$E_{13} = \frac{+5.7 - 5.0 + 12.1 - 11.1 - 5.7 + 5.0 - 12.1 + 11.1}{4} = 0.0$$

Machine Quantity & Rework Rate E_{23}

$$E_{23} = \frac{+5.7 + 5.0 - 12.1 - 11.1 - 5.7 - 5.0 + 12.1 + 11.1}{4} = 0.0$$

Table T11.12D displays example calculations for the interactive effects in the previous example. All interactive effects (E_{12}, E_{13}, E_{23}) in this example are inconsequential because their values are very low. Hence, we can conclude that there is strong evidence that the main effects are entirely induced from the mere changing of the respective factor levels.

The different effects that are calculated are assumed to be random variables from an unknown distribution whose true mean is μ. Point estimates of μ (e.g., $\overline{E}_{12}(n)$) are assumed to come from a normally distributed sample population when the sample size n is large. Therefore, confidence intervals can be established by utilizing previously described methods.

The theory behind factorial experiments and other experimental design techniques can not be fully explained in three or four pages. The information presented in this book only provides the reader with elementary facts regarding basic concepts and procedures.

The mathematical equations used in the statistical analyses may appear intimidating to those who are not familiar with statistical notations. In reality, the math is fairly simple. However, performing the computations manually can be a very tedious task. A computer can do the job much faster and more efficiently.

An unfamiliarity with statistics should not discourage someone from using simulation. Many simulation packages contain features that will automatically perform basic statistical analyses on simulation output. The important thing is to have a fundamental knowledge of the various statistical analyses, and their purpose.

Chapter 11.13

IDENTIFY BEST SOLUTIONS AND DOCUMENT RESULTS

STEPS TO CONDUCTING A SUCCESSFUL SIMULATION PROJECT
1. Formulate And Analyze The Problem
2. Educate The Team On Basic Simulation Principles
3. Develop Model Concept
4. Macro Data Collection
5. Model Concept And Macro Data Review
6. Construct The Model
7. Model Verification
8. Test The Model With Macro Data
9. Model Validation
10. Design Experiments For Evaluating Alternatives
11. Make Multiple Model Runs For Each Alternative
12. Statistical Analysis Of Output
13. Identify Best Solutions And Document Results
14. Presentation Of Results And Implementation

Identify Best Solutions And Document Results

- Documentation Requirements

- Objectives And Assumptions

- Model Input Parameters

- Model Verification And Validation

- Experimental Design

- Results

- Conclusions And Recommendations

Documentation Requirements

Documentation can be divided into six areas, **1) Objectives and Assumptions, 2) Model Input Parameters, 4) Experimental Design, 5) Results, and 6) Conclusions**. If the model building steps described in chapter 11, *"Conducting A Successful Simulation Project,"* are adhered to, then the bulk of this task is already completed. All that remains is to put the information into a presentable report format.

Objectives and Assumptions - All objectives and assumptions should be recorded at the onset of any simulation project. Any changes or modifications made during the course of building a model need to be included in the final report. This section should also contain reasons for **why** the study was initiated.

Model Input Parameters - This section contains a description of how the model was developed and a recap of the data used with it. How were the various components of the system modeled? What data was used and where did it come from? System flow charts, mathematical calculations, performance criteria, solution constraints, solution restrictions, and any cost related information should be reported. Variable and attribute dictionaries should also be included.

Model Verification And Validation - Methods used for model verification and validation should be noted in the final documentation. This can include a listing of the model coding that has been checked by an independent party to verify that all model conditions and input parameters have been properly incorporated into the model. The procedures used to validate the model should also be explained.

Experimental Design - The information summarized in this category is comprised of descriptions regarding the alternatives investigated, the experiments designed for comparing alternatives, starting conditions, stopping conditions, a history of the random number streams employed with each experiment, and an account for the number of model replications performed for each alternative.

Results - This section is composed of the output data produced by a simulation. It also provides an overview of the statistical analyses performed on the data. This includes the determination of warm-up periods and confidence intervals. Tables and graphical charts that illustrate the findings are very beneficial.

Conclusions And Recommendations - One of the final steps in any decision-making process is to make conclusions and recommendations. This demands that benefit-to-cost ratios be investigated for each alternative. What are the total costs (tangible and intangible) needed to implement an alternative, and what are the total benefits anticipated from doing it? Sometimes this is referred to as an ROI (Return On Investment) analysis. Payback periods and internal rate of returns are examples of other financial analyses that are used for evaluating alternatives. Chapter 14, *"Assessing The Savings From Simulation,"* discusses some of these methods in greater detail. They can be very beneficial when presenting recommendations to management.

Since decision-making is based on the precept of prediction, risks and uncertainties are almost always involved. The potential labor requirements forecasted with a given alternative may fall within a range. This can be classified as an uncertainty. The potential outcome for an alternative may also vary. This can be designated as a risk. Any uncertainties and risks associated with an alternative should be discussed in the final documentation.

Chapter 11.14

PRESENTATION OF RESULTS AND IMPLEMENTATION

STEPS TO CONDUCTING A SUCCESSFUL SIMULATION PROJECT
1. Formulate And Analyze The Problem
2. Educate The Team On Basic Simulation Principles
3. Develop Model Concept
4. Macro Data Collection
5. Model Concept And Macro Data Review
6. Construct The Model
7. Model Verification
8. Test The Model With Macro Data
9. Model Validation
10. Design Experiments For Evaluating Alternatives
11. Make Multiple Model Runs For Each Alternative
12. Statistical Analysis Of Output
13. Identify Best Solutions And Document Results
14. Presentation Of Results And Implementation

Presentation Of Results And Implementation

- Project "Team" Presentation

- Who Should Attend?

- What Should Be Presented?

- Implementation-Follow-up